CHINESE COOKING

THE COMPLETE BOOK OF
CHINESE COOKING

Edited by
Veronica Sperling & Christine McFadden

SMITHMARK

Distributed in the USA by SMITHMARK Publishers,
a division of U.S. Media Holdings Inc.,
16, East 32nd Street, New York, NY 10016

First published in the UK in 1996

SMITHMARK books are available for bulk purchase for sales promotion and premium
use. For details, write or call the manager of special sales, SMITHMARK publishers,
16 East 32nd Street, New York, NY 10016; (212) 532-6600

ISBN: 0-76519-684-0

10 9 8 7 6 5 4 3 2 1

Printed in Italy

Produced by Haldane Mason, London

Acknowledgements
Art Direction: Ron Samuels
Design: Digital Artworks Partnership Ltd

Material contained in this book has previously appeared in
Chinese Cantonese Cooking and *Chinese Szechuan Cooking* by Deh-Ta Hsiung
Vegetarian Chinese Cooking and *Microwave Meals* by Wendy Lee
Wok Cooking by Rosemary Wadey
Thai Cooking by Carol Bowen
Quick & Easy Meals by Carole Handslip

Contents

INTRODUCTION 6

APPETIZERS 18

SALADS & PICKLES 40

SOUPS 54

FISH & SEAFOOD 86

POULTRY DISHES 114

MEAT DISHES 140

VEGETABLE DISHES 172

RICE DISHES 216

NOODLE DISHES 238

INDEX 254

CHINESE CUISINE

From the hot, spicy dishes of Szechuan to the aromatic crispy duck of Beijing, the cooking of China offers a fascinating range of delicious dishes for you to create in your own kitchen. Once you have mastered one or two simple basic principles, you'll appreciate the speed and ease with which Chinese food can be cooked, whether it is for a complete meal or as an accompaniment to your normal food.

THE CHINESE DIET

With its wealth of foodstuffs and distinctive regional cooking styles, it's little wonder that China claims to have the world's most diverse cuisine. Yet the fundamental character of Chinese cooking remains the same throughout the land: from Peking in the north to Canton in the south, and from Shanghai in the east to Szechuan in the west, different ingredients are prepared, cooked, and served in accordance with centuries-old principles. Some of the cooking methods may vary a little from one region to another, and the emphasis on seasonings may differ, but basically dishes from different regions are all unmistakably 'Chinese'.

A HEALTHY OPTION

The variety of Chinese cooking appeals to people in every corner of the globe, not only because of the range of unusual and exotic ingredients but because the daily diet is one of the healthiest in the world. It is based largely on vegetables and carbohydrates (such as rice or noodles) with only a little fish or meat. Dairy products are not used.

THE VEGETARIAN ELEMENT

Widespread poverty means that many people are unable to afford meat, and many follow a vegetarian diet for religious reasons. In addition, the selection of vegetables available in the markets has increased in recent years as China's peasants have been encouraged to grow their own crops. But even when they have the choice, the Chinese have many reasons for eating more vegetarian food than other kinds. They recognize not only that a mainly vegetarian diet is the healthiest way to eat, but that it is also more economical to use the land for growing vegetables and rice than for grazing livestock, as the crops will feed infinitely more people.

REGIONAL COOKING

Being such a vast country – about the same size as the United States – China encompasses a number of different climates. Even though it lies mainly within the temperate zone both geographically and climatically, the regions are widely diverse. From the Tibetan Plateau in the west (12,000 feet), the country descends eastward to the Yangtze flood plain. It is the diversity of the countryside that has given rise to the wide variety of produce and the great range of regional cooking styles.

China breaks down into four distinct regions, each of which has its own style of cuisine and specialties.

Cantonese (Southern School)

This is the best-known cuisine in the western world because of the large numbers of Chinese who emigrated from Canton to Europe and America in the nineteenth century. Also, because Canton was the first Chinese port opened for trade, it is the most influenced by foreign

contact and offers the widest variety of food. Light and subtle flavorings are used and the food is less fatty than in other regions. The region is famous for its seafood specialties, as well as its sweet and sour dishes and crispy pork recipes.

Peking (Northern School)

The staple food is mainly wheat and corn, rather than rice, with an emphasis on noodles, dumplings, and pancakes. Due to the harsh winter, many food products are preserved by drying, smoking, or pickling.

Szechuan (Western School)

The Szechuan cuisine is characterized by its dependence on strong flavorings and hot spices such as red chilies, Szechuan peppercorns, ginger, and garlic. Pungent vegetables, such as garlic, onions, and scallions, are used in large quantities. Nuts add richness and flavor to dishes, while aromatic ground rice and sesame seeds are often used to coat meat prior to deep-frying or stir-frying. Sesame paste is often the principal ingredient in sauces. The region is also noted for its food preservation techniques, which include salting, drying, smoking, and pickling, probably because the humid climate makes it difficult to keep food fresh.

Shanghai (Eastern School)

This region is rich in fruit and vegetables, and is well known for its vegetarian cuisine as well as its fresh fish. Sugar and oil are used in large quantities, earning the area a reputation for rich food.

THE PRINCIPLES OF CHINESE COOKING

What distinguishes Chinese cooking from all other food cultures is the emphasis on the harmonious blending of color, aroma, flavor, and texture, both in a single dish and in all the dishes which make up the meal. Consciously or unconsciously, Chinese cooks,

from the housewife to the professional chef, all work to this ancient Taoist principle of Yin and Yang in which balance and contrast are the key.

In order to achieve this, two most important factors should be observed, that is, heat and timing – the degree of heat and duration of cooking, which means the right cooking method for the right food. This is why the size and shape of the cut ingredient must, first of all, be suitable for a particular method of cooking. For instance, ingredients for quick stir-frying should be cut into small, thin slices or shreds of uniform size, never into large, thick chunks. This is not just for the sake of appearance, but also because ingredients of the same size and shape require about the same amount of cooking time.

Bear these general points in mind when you cook Chinese food and you will find it surprisingly easy to create delicious dishes that are also a visual delight.

The recipes in this book have been designed to achieve exactly this. They are quick and simple to prepare and they mostly use ingredients obtainable from supermarkets. Occasionally, you may need to visit a Chinese food store to find one or two ingredients. Some of the recipes have been adapted for the vegetarian from traditional Chinese recipes, and others are vegetarian dishes that have been developed to suit the Western kitchen.

CHINESE MEALS

Meal times in China are often family gatherings at which many different dishes are served. A wide range of ingredients is used, but the different flavors of the many dishes are always made to work together. The meal is served all at once, including the soup. Unlike the Western convention, the Chinese never serve an individual dish to each person; all the dishes on the table are shared.

The Chinese do not usually have desserts to finish off a meal, except at banquets and special occasions. Sweet dishes are usually served in between main meals as snacks, but fruit is refreshing at the end of a big meal.

MENU PLANNING

When planning a menu for a shared meal, allow one dish per person. For example, if you are cooking for only two or three people, serve one main dish with one vegetable side dish and one rice or noodle dish, plus a soup if desired. For an informal meal for four to six people, serve four dishes plus soup and rice; for a formal dinner for approximately the same number of people, allow a range of six to eight dishes. Always increase the number of dishes rather than the quantity of ingredients when cooking for many people, as this will give more variety and contrast of taste, color, and flavor on the table.

Do not choose too many dishes that need a lot of last-minute preparation or have to be served immediately, such as stir-fries. Vary the dishes so that some may be prepared in advance, and then you too can enjoy the meal and not spend all evening in the kitchen.

TEA DRINKING

In China, tea is unlikely to be drunk during the actual meal, as it is generally the custom to place a bowl of clear soup on the table instead for the duration of the meal. Tea is then served at the end of the meal as it is considered to be both refreshing and invigorating.

Tea has been known as a drink in China certainly for more than 2,000 years and probably much longer. However, it was not until the eighth century that tea became a common drink, popular with all classes of people. Today, tea drinking is a part of everyday life in China and a pot of strong tea is kept warm all day to provide a regular supply.

To the tea connoisseur, the tradition of tea drinking is, as it has always been through the ages, akin to a religious ritual and a return to nature and purity. Ideally, preparing tea should be carried out under immaculate and tranquil conditions. The setting is especially important and should be as peaceful as possible; in fact, the ideal place is considered to be on a mountain so that, as an additional benefit, mountain water is used for the tea.

WINE

Many European and New World wines blend well with Chinese food, particularly the light, dry whites and lighter Burgundy-style reds. Chinese wine is an acquired taste. Being mostly made with fermented rice, it has a very different flavor from wine made with grapes. The best-known Chinese wine is called Shaoxing, which is also used in cooking.

GLOSSARY OF INGREDIENTS

The list covers the most commonly used ingredients in Chinese cooking. These ingredients are becoming much more widely available, particularly in the supermarkets, health food shops, and Chinese stores. Substitutes can often be used for the more unusual ingredients.

Baby corncobs

Baby corncobs have a wonderfully sweet flavor and irresistible texture. They are available both fresh and canned.

Bamboo shoots

Available in cans only. Once opened, the contents may be kept in fresh water in a covered jar in the refrigerator for up to a week.

Bean curd

This custard-like preparation of puréed and pressed yellow soybeans is exceptionally high in protein. Bean curd has a distinctive texture but a bland flavor. It is usually sold in two forms: in cakes about 3 inches square and 1 in. thick or as a semi-thick jelly. There is also a dried form, which is sold in oriental and health food stores. For solid tofu, use a sharp knife to cut the required amount into cubes or shreds. Cook carefully as it will break up if stirred too much. Tofu will keep for a few days in the refrigerator if put in a sealed container and submerged in water.

Bean-sprouts

Fresh bean-sprouts, from mung or soybeans, are widely available from oriental stores and supermarkets. They can be kept in the refrigerator for 2–3 days.

Bean sauce

Available in black or yellow, bean sauce is made from crushed salted soybeans mixed with flour and spices (such as ginger or chili) to make a thickish paste. It is used for flavoring dishes or as a condiment. The sauce is sold in cans or jars and once opened should be stored in the refrigerator.

Black beans

Salted fermented soybeans, available in packets or cans.

Chili bean sauce

Fermented bean paste mixed with hot chilies and other seasonings. Sold in jars, some sauces are quite mild, but others are very hot. You will have to try out the various brands to see which one is to your taste.

Chilies

These can be red or green, and come in a variety of sizes – the smaller the chili, the hotter it is, and dried chilies are often hotter than fresh. Take care when handling them, as chili juice stings; avoid touching your eyes and always wash your hands thoroughly afterwards. Discard the seeds, as these are the hottest part.

Chili oil

A very hot chili-flavored red oil; use sparingly. You can make your own by adding a few dried chilies to a small bottle of oil. Leave them to soak for a few days to allow the flavor to develop.

Chili sauce

Very hot sauce made from chilies, vinegar, sugar, and salt. Usually sold in bottles and should be used sparingly in cooking or as a dip. Tabasco sauce can be used as a substitute if you do not happen to have the real thing.

Chinese leaves

Also known as Chinese cabbage and bok choy, there are two widely available varieties to be found in supermarkets and vegetable stores. The most common is pale green with a tightly wrapped, elongated head. Roughly two-thirds of the cabbage consists of crunchy-textured stem. The other variety has a shorter, fatter head with curlier, pale yellow or green leaves with white stems.

Cilantro

Fresh cilantro leaves, also known as Chinese parsley, have a distinctive flavor. Cilantro is widely used in Chinese cooking. It can be chopped and added to sauces and stuffing. The feathery leaves make an attractive garnish. Parsley can be used as a substitute.

Dried Chinese mushrooms

Highly fragrant dried mushrooms which add a special flavor to Chinese dishes. There are many different varieties, but shiitake are the best. They are not cheap, but a small amount will go a long way, and they will keep indefinitely in an airtight jar.

Soak them in warm water for 20–30 minutes (or in cold water for several hours), squeeze dry, and discard the hard stems before use.

Egg noodles

There are many varieties of egg noodles in China, ranging from flat, broad ribbons to long, narrow strands. Both dried and fresh egg noodles are readily available.

Five-spice powder

This is a mixture of star anise, fennel seeds, cloves, cinnamon bark, and Szechuan pepper. It is very pungent so should only be used sparingly. It will keep in an airtight container indefinitely.

Garlic

A primary seasoning in Chinese food that not only adds flavor but has health-giving properties. Garlic may be chopped, crushed, or pickled and is very often used in sauces and stuffings.

Store garlic in a cool, dry area, not in the refrigerator where it will go moldy.

Ginger root

Fresh ginger root, sold by the weight, should be peeled and then sliced, finely chopped, or shredded before use. It will keep for several weeks in a dry, cool place. Dried ginger powder is not a good substitute.

Hoi-sin sauce

Also known as barbecue sauce, this is made from soybeans, sugar, flour, vinegar, salt, garlic, chili, and sesame seed oil. Sold in cans or jars, it will keep in the refrigerator for several months.

Lemon grass

An aromatic herb, available as fresh stems or dried as powder. Chop or slice the lower part of the stem to use.

Lotus leaves

Leaves of the lotus plant. They are very large and sold dried. Soak in hot water before use. These are often used as a shell in which other ingredients are cooked, such as steamed rice.

Noodles

Made from rice, pulses, or wheat. There is a large variety available, all of which can be interchanged in recipes. Cook according to packet instructions.

Oils

The most commonly used oil in Chinese cooking is groundnut oil. It has a light flavor and can be heated without smoking to a higher temperature than most oils. It is therefore especially useful for stir-frying and deep-frying. Rape or sunflower oils are also popular, while butter is never used, and lard and chicken fat only occasionally.

Oyster sauce

A thickish soy-based sauce used as a flavoring in Cantonese cooking. It will keep in the refrigerator for months.

Plum sauce

Plum sauce has a unique, fruity flavor – a sweet and sour sauce with a difference.

Rice vinegar

There are two basic types of rice vinegar. Red vinegar is made from fermented rice and has a distinctive dark color and depth of flavor. White vinegar is stronger in flavor as it is distilled from rice wine.

Rice wine

Chinese rice wine, made from glutinous rice, is also known as yellow wine (*huang jiu* or *chiew* in Chinese), because of its golden color. The best variety, from south-east China, is called Shao Hsing or Shaoxing. A good dry or medium sherry can be an acceptable substitute.

Sesame oil

Aromatic oil sold in bottles and widely used as a finishing touch, added to dishes just before serving. The refined yellow sesame oil sold in Middle Eastern stores is not so aromatic, has less flavor, and therefore is not a very satisfactory substitute.

Sesame seeds

These add texture and a nutty flavor to dishes. Dry-fry to add color and accentuate the flavor.

Sherry

If rice wine is difficult to obtain, a good quality dry pale sherry can be used instead. Sweet sherry should not be substituted.

Soy sauce

Sold in bottles or cans, this popular Chinese sauce is used both for cooking and at the table. Light soy sauce has more flavor than the sweeter, dark soy sauce, which gives the food a rich, reddish color.

Straw mushrooms

Grown on beds of rice straw, hence the name, straw mushrooms have a pleasant slippery texture and a subtle taste. Canned straw mushrooms should be rinsed and drained after opening.

Szechuan peppercorns

Also known as *farchiew*, these are wild reddish-brown peppercorns from Szechuan. More aromatic but less hot than either white or black peppercorns, they give a unique and delicious flavor to a variety of dishes.

Szechuan preserved vegetable

This is a speciality of the Szechuan province. It is the root of a special variety of the mustard green pickled in salt and hot chili. Sold in cans, once opened it can be stored in a sealed jar in the refrigerator for months.

Tiger lily buds

Also known as golden needles, these are dried lily-flower buds. Soak in water before use.

Tree ears

Also known as cloud ears, this is a dried black fungus. Sold in plastic bags in oriental stores, they should be soaked in cold or warm water for 20 minutes, then rinsed in fresh water before use. Tree ears have a crunchy texture and mild but subtle flavor. Fresh 'Jews ears' fungi are a good substitute.

Water chestnuts

The roots of the plant *Heleocharis tuberosa*. Also known as horse's hooves in China on account of their appearance before the skin is peeled off. They are available fresh or in cans. Canned water chestnuts retain only part of the texture, and even less of the flavor of fresh ones. They will keep for a month in the refrigerator in a covered jar, changing the water every two or three days.

Wonton skins or wrappers

These are made from flour, egg, and water. They can be deep-fried and served with a dipping sauce, or they may be filled with a range of mixtures prior to deep-frying, steaming, or boiling.

You can buy them ready-made or make your own. Layers of filo pastry make a reasonable substitute. They can be kept frozen for up to six months.

EQUIPMENT

Chinese utensils are of an ancient design and are usually made of inexpensive materials. They have been in continuous use for thousands of years and do serve a special function. Their more sophisticated and expensive Western counterparts sometimes prove rather inadequate in contrast.

Chinese cleaver

Good, strong, sharp kitchen knives are more than adequate but it is worth trying to work with a Chinese cleaver. The wide blade looks clumsy, but the corner of the blade can do anything the point of a knife can do. Also, the blade can be used to carry the chopped ingredients to the cooking pot.

Cleavers vary in weight and thickness of blade. The heavier type is used for chopping through bones, while the lighter, sharper type is ideal for delicate, precision work.

Chopsticks

Does Chinese food taste any better when eaten with chopsticks? This is not merely an aesthetic question, but also a practical point, partly because all Chinese food is prepared in such a way that it is easily picked up by chopsticks.

Learning to use chopsticks is quite easy – simply place one chopstick in the hollow between thumb and index finger and rest its lower end below the first joint of the third finger. This chopstick remains stationary. Hold the other chopstick between the tips of the index and middle fingers, steady its upper half against the base of the index finger, and use the tip of the thumb to keep it in place. To pick up food, move the upper chopstick with index and middle fingers. When eating rice and other difficult-to-hold foods, it is better to lift the bowl to the chin and then push the food into the mouth using the chopsticks as a type of shovel, as the Chinese do.

Chopsticks are also used in food preparation, as they make an excellent tool for stirring, whipping, and beating the ingredients prior to cooking. They can be bought in most cookshops and from many Chinese restaurants.

Ladle and spatula

Wok sets usually consist of a pair of stirrers in the form of a ladle and spatula. Of the two, the flat ladle or scooper (as it is sometimes called) is more versatile. It is used by the Chinese cook for adding ingredients and seasonings to the wok, besides being a stirring implement.

Steamers

Steaming can be done in any covered pot large enough to take a plate placed on a rack set over boiling water. There should be space for the steam to circulate. The food is put on the plate and a well-fitting lid put on top. A wok with its own lid will serve very well. The traditional Chinese steamer is made of bamboo; the modern version is made of aluminum.

Bamboo steamers are particularly suited to the technique as the gaps in the bamboo allow excess steam to escape. They are designed to stand one on top of another, enabling you to cook several dishes at the same time. They can be bought in a range of sizes at Chinese specialty shops or good cookware shops.

Wok

The round-bottomed iron wok conducts and retains heat evenly. Because of its shape, the ingredients always return to the center, where the heat is most intense, however vigorously you stir. The wok is also ideal for deep-frying – its conical shape requires far less oil than a flat-bottomed deep-fryer. It has more depth (which means more heat) and more cooking surface (which means more food can be cooked at one go). Besides being a skillet, a wok is also used for braising, steaming, boiling, and poaching – in other words, the whole spectrum of Chinese cooking methods can be executed in one single utensil.

It is essential that a new iron wok is seasoned properly before use. Prepare it by washing thoroughly in hot water and detergent then drying it well. To season, put the wok over a gentle heat and, when the metal heats up, wipe over the entire inner surface with a pad of paper towels that you have first dipped in oil. Repeat the process using fresh oiled paper until the paper stays clean.

Clean the wok after each use by washing it with water, using a mild detergent if necessary, and a soft cloth or brush. Do not scrub or use any abrasive cleaner as this will scratch the surface. Dry thoroughly with paper towels or over a low heat, then wipe the surface all over with a little oil. This forms a sealing layer to protect the surface of the wok from moisture and thus helps to prevent it from rusting.

GARNISHES

Chinese food should always be pleasing to the eye as well as the palate. The dishes can be intricately decorated with delicately cut vegetables, adding color as well as a finishing touch. The garnishes can be as simple or elaborate as you wish, depending on time and patience. The simpler garnishes could be sprigs of fresh or chopped herbs, such as cilantro, chervil, or chives, shreds of scallion, chili, lemon zest or radish, or twists of lime or lemon. Some more elaborate garnishes are described below. Experiment with both for the best results.

Cucumber fans

Cut a piece of cucumber about 3 inches long and divide this in half lengthwise. Lay a piece of cucumber cut side down and, using a small, sharp knife, cut thin slices along the length to within ½ in. of the end. Carefully turn alternate slices over in half and tuck in. Place in iced water until required.

Carrot flowers

Peel the carrot. Using a sharp knife, make about five or six tiny V-shaped cuts along the length. Then cut into slices: the V-shapes will ensure each slice looks like a flower petal.

Fresh chili flowers

Trim the tip of the chili but do not remove the skin. Make four cuts lengthwise from the stem of the chili to the tip to make four sections. Remove and discard any seeds. Soak the chilies in cold water – they will flower in the water.

Radish flowers

Trim each end of the radish. Using a sharp knife, make V-shaped cuts around the top and remove the cut parts to expose the white of the radish.

Radish roses

For radish roses, trim the ends, then hold the knife flat to the radish skin and make short vertical cuts around the sides, as if you were shaving off the outer skin, but without detaching each 'petal'. Plunge straight into iced water.

Shrimp crackers

These are compressed slivers of shrimp and flour paste which expand into large, translucent chips when deep-fried.

Tomato roses

For tomato roses, peel off the skin of a tomato in one long strip using a sharp knife. Curl the skin into a circle.

COOKING TECHNIQUES

Chinese food generally takes much longer to prepare than it does to cook, so it is very important to prepare each dish as much in advance as possible. Ensure all the vegetables are chopped and the sauces blended before you start cooking.

Chopping

Cut the ingredients into small, uniformly sized pieces to ensure that the food cooks evenly. Shredding vegetables thinly and slicing them diagonally ensures fast cooking, as it increases the area in contact with the hot oil.

Stir-frying

This is the method of cooking most commonly associated with Chinese cuisine. The correct piece of equipment for this is a wok (page 13) as it gives the best results. However, any large skillet or heavy saucepan will do.

Stir-frying with a wok is a very healthy way to cook, as it uses very little oil and preserves the nutrients in the food. It is very important that the wok is very hot before you begin to cook. This can be tested by holding your hand flat about 3 inches over the base of the interior, when you will feel the heat radiating from it. The success of stir-frying lies in having the wok at just the right temperature, and in ensuring correct timing when cooking the food.

Before cooking commences, ensure that all the required ingredients are prepared, ready to be added to the wok the instant the oil is the right heat. Cooking at too low a temperature or for too long will produce inferior results.

Add a small amount of oil to the wok and heat it, then add, in stages, the various ingredients to be cooked – those requiring longer cooking go in first, while those that require only very little cooking go in last.

Using a long-handled metal or wooden spoon or flat scoop, constantly stir the ingredients for a very short time. This ensures that all the ingredients come into contact with the hot oil so the natural juices of the food are sealed in, leaving it crisp and colorful. The technique also ensures that all the ingredients are evenly cooked. Stir-fried dishes look and taste best when served immediately.

Deep-frying

Use a wok, a deep-fryer, or a heavy-based saucepan. When deep-frying in a wok, use enough oil to give a depth of about 2 inches. Heat it over a moderate heat until you can see a faint haze of smoke rising before gently lowering in the food to be fried. Make sure the oil is up to temperature before adding the food so that the hot oil cooks the food quickly on the outside, forming a protective seal. If the oil is not hot enough, the food will act like a sponge and becoming soggy and greasy. Before frying the food, make sure that it is dry in order to prevent the oil from splattering. If the food has been marinated, let it drain well. If it is in batter, wait for it to stop dripping.

Cook the food in small batches so as not to overcrowd the wok or skillet, as this can reduce the temperature of the oil and lead to unevenly cooked food. Always remove the food from the oil with a perforated spoon and drain thoroughly on paper towels to absorb any excess oil. Once it has been strained, cooking oil can be reused up to three times, but only for the same type of food.

Steaming

This is another very popular Chinese cooking method. There are two methods of steaming. In the first, the food is arranged on a plate or bowl which is then put inside a steamer on a perforated rack and placed over a large pot of boiling water. The plate or bowl can also be put inside a wok. The steam passes through the steamer and cooks the food. Larger items of food, such as dumplings, can be placed straight onto the rack or laid on cabbage leaves or soaked lotus leaves. The leaves not only prevent the food from falling through, but also add extra flavor.

In the second method, the bowl of ingredients is partially immersed in boiling water. The food is cooked partly by the boiling water and partly by the steam it produces.

Braising and red braising

This method is similar to Western braising and is generally used for cooking tougher cuts of meat and firm varieties of vegetables. The ingredients are stir-fried until lightly brown. Stock is added and brought to a boil. The heat is then reduced to simmering until cooking is complete. Red braising uses the same method but the food is braised in a reddish-brown liquid, such as soy sauce. This sauce can be re-used.

BASIC RECIPES

Common to many recipes are standard preparations such as stock, plain boiled rice, and cornstarch paste. Dipping sauces are also served with many dishes.

Chinese Stock

This basic stock is used not only as the basis for soup-making, but also for general use in Chinese cooking. It will keep for up to 4–5 days in the refrigerator. Alternatively, it can be frozen in small containers and defrosted as required. These quantities make 10 cups.

1½ lb chicken pieces
1½ lb pork sparerib
15 cups cold water
3–4 pieces ginger root, crushed
3–4 scallions, each tied into a knot
3–4 tbsp Chinese rice wine or dry sherry

Trim off excess fat from the chicken and sparerib, then chop them into large pieces. Put in a large pan with the water, ginger, and scallion knots. Bring to a boil, and skim off the scum. Reduce the heat and simmer uncovered for at least 2–3 hours.
   Strain the stock, discarding the chicken, pork, ginger, and scallions. Pour back in the pan and add the wine. Bring to a boil, then simmer for 2–3 minutes. Allow to cool, then store in the refrigerator.

Cornstarch Paste

Cornstarch paste is made by mixing 1 part cornstarch with about 1.5 parts of cold water. Stir until smooth. Use to thicken sauces.

Plain Rice

Use long-grain or patna rice, or better still, try Thai fragrant rice. This amount serves 4.

1¼ cups long-grain rice
about 1 cup cold water
pinch of salt
½ tsp oil (optional)

Wash and rinse the rice just once. Place the rice in a saucepan and add enough water so that there is no more than ¹/₂ in. of water above the surface of the rice. Bring to a boil, add salt and oil (if using), and stir once to prevent the rice sticking to the bottom of the pan.
   Reduce the heat to very, very low. Cover and cook for 15–20 minutes. Remove from the heat and let stand, covered, for 10 minutes or so. Fluff up the rice with a fork or spoon before serving.

DIPPING SAUCES

Traditional sauces for Chinese food include the following.

Sweet & Sour Sauce

A tasty sweet and sour sauce which goes well with many deep-fried foods. Store in a well-sealed container in the refrigerator. It will keep well.

2 tbsp ginger marmalade
2 tbsp orange marmalade
¼ tsp salt
1 tbsp white rice vinegar (or cider vinegar)
1 tbsp hot water

Combine all the ingredients in a small bowl, mixing well. Serve in a small bowl.

Salt & Pepper Sauce

A roasted salt and pepper mixture made with Szechuan peppercorns is found throughout China as a dip for deep-fried foods. The dry-roasting method brings out all the flavors of the peppercorns.

2 oz Szechuan peppercorns
3 oz coarse sea salt

Put a heavy skillet over medium heat. Add the peppercorns and the salt and stir-fry until the mixture begins to brown. Remove the skillet from the heat and let the mixture cool. Grind the mixture in a grinder or with a pestle and mortar.

Scallion Sauce

Heated oil poured over the seasonings brings out their full flavor. The sauce goes well with meat and poultry dishes.

3 tbsp finely chopped scallions
3 tbsp finely grated fresh ginger root
2 tsp salt
1 tsp light soy sauce
3 tbsp oil (groundnut or sunflower)

Place the scallions, ginger root, salt, and soy sauce in a small heatproof bowl. Put the oil into a small saucepan and heat over a moderate heat until it begins to smoke.

Remove the oil from the heat and pour over the seasonings. Leave the sauce to stand for at least 2–3 hours before using, to allow the flavors to blend.

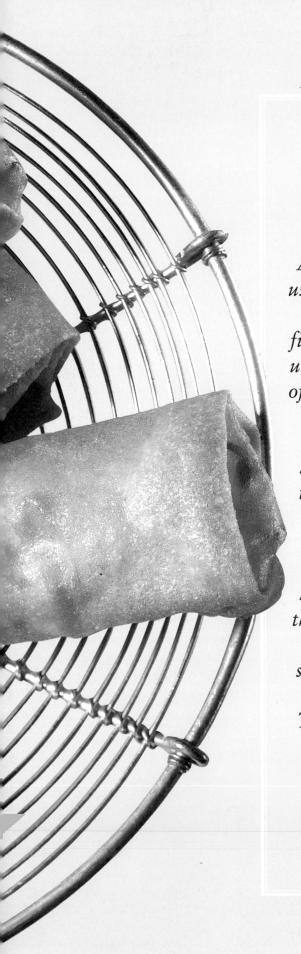

APPETIZERS

A selection of small portions of several different dishes usually starts the Chinese meal - just like hors d'oeuvres in the West. Many of these appetizers consist of tasty fillings enclosed in pastry-type wrappers which are fried until crisp. These are served with a simple dipping sauce of soy sauce, sherry, and strips of scallion and chili. Spicy deep-fried shrimp, or bite-size sparerib, or pieces of chicken are also popular.

Serve an assortment of appetizers with a minimum of three different items, but remember not to have more than one of the same type of food. The ingredients should be chosen for their harmony and balance in color, aroma, texture, and flavor.

Snacks and appetizers are sold at many roadside stalls throughout China, and are bought and eaten by people as they go about their daily tasks. After dusk, the sidewalks are filled with groups of families and friends cooking, eating, and selling many delicious meals.

This is an important part of their social lives, and is an enjoyable way of getting together and sharing food.

Crispy Wontons with Piquant Dipping Sauce

Mushroom-filled crispy wontons are served on skewers with a chili-flavored dipping sauce.

SERVES 4

INGREDIENTS

1 tbsp vegetable oil
1 tbsp chopped onion
1 small garlic clove, chopped
½ tsp chopped ginger root
½ cup flat mushrooms, chopped
16 wonton skins
vegetable oil for deep-frying
salt

SAUCE

2 tbsp vegetable oil
2 scallions, shredded thinly
1 red and 1 green chili,
deseeded and shredded thinly
3 tbsp light soy sauce
1 tbsp vinegar
1 tbsp dry sherry
pinch of sugar

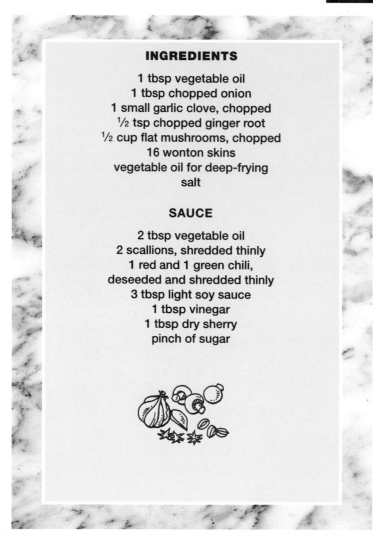

1 Heat the oil in a wok or skillet. Add the onion, garlic, and ginger root, and stir-fry for 2 minutes. Stir in the mushrooms and fry for a further 2 minutes. Season well with salt and leave to cool.

2 Place 1 teaspoon of the cooled mushroom filling in the center of each wonton skin. Bring two opposite corners together to cover the mixture and pinch together to seal. Repeat with the remaining corners.

3 Thread the wontons onto 8 wooden skewers. Heat enough oil in a large saucepan to deep-fry the wontons in batches until golden and crisp. Remove with a perforated spoon and drain on paper towels.

4 To make the sauce, heat the oil in a small saucepan until quite hot, i.e. until a small cube of bread dropped in the oil browns in a few seconds. Put the scallions and chilies in a bowl and pour the hot oil slowly on top. Then mix in the remaining ingredients and serve with the crispy wontons.

Step *1*

Step *2*

Step *4*

Crispy Seaweed

Popular in many Chinese restaurants, this dish is served as a starter.
This 'seaweed' is, in fact, deep-fried spring greens.

SERVES 4

INGREDIENTS

8 oz spring greens
vegetable oil for deep-frying
1½ tsp superfine sugar
1 tsp salt
¼ cup slivered almonds

1 Wash the spring greens thoroughly. Trim off the excess tough stalks. Place on paper towels or a dry dishcloth and leave to drain thoroughly.

2 Using a sharp knife, shred the spring greens very finely, then spread out the shreds on paper towels for about 30 minutes to dry.

3 Heat the oil in a wok or deep-fat fryer. Remove the pan from the heat and add the spring greens in batches. Return the pan to the heat and deep-fry until the greens begin to float to the surface and become translucent and crinkled. Remove with a perforated spoon, and drain on paper towels. Keep each batch warm.

4 Mix the sugar and salt together, sprinkle over the 'seaweed', and toss together to mix well.

5 Add the slivered almonds to the hot oil and fry until lightly golden. Remove with a perforated spoon and drain on paper towels.

6 Serve the crispy 'seaweed' with the slivered almonds.

Step *2*

Step *3*

Step *4*

Spring Rolls

Thin slices of vegetables are wrapped in pastry and deep-fried until crisp.
Spring roll wrappers are available from oriental shops and some supermarkets.

MAKES 12

INGREDIENTS

5 Chinese dried mushrooms
(or open-cup mushrooms)
1 large carrot
1 cup canned bamboo shoots
2 scallions
2 oz Chinese leaves
2 tbsp vegetable oil
4 cups bean-sprouts
1 tbsp soy sauce
12 spring roll wrappers
1 egg, beaten
vegetable oil for deep-frying
salt

1 Place the dried mushrooms in a small bowl and cover with warm water. Leave to soak for 20–25 minutes. Drain the mushrooms and squeeze out the excess water. Remove the tough centers and then slice the mushrooms thinly.

2 Cut the carrot and bamboo shoots into very thin julienne strips. Chop the scallions and shred the Chinese leaves.

3 Heat the 2 tablespoons of oil in a wok or skillet. Add the mushrooms, carrot, and bamboo shoots, and stir-fry for 2 minutes. Add the scallions, Chinese leaves, bean-sprouts, and soy sauce. Season with salt and stir-fry for 2 minutes. Leave to cool.

4 Divide the mixture into 12 equal portions and place one portion on the edge of each spring roll wrapper. Fold in the sides and roll each one up, brushing the join with a little beaten egg to seal.

5 Deep-fry the spring rolls in batches in hot oil in a wok or large saucepan for 4–5 minutes, or until golden and crisp. Take care that the oil is not too hot or the spring rolls will brown on the outside before cooking on the inside. Remove and drain on paper towels. Keep each batch of spring rolls warm while the others are being cooked. Serve at once.

Step *2*

Step *4*

Step *5*

Lettuce-Wrapped Ground Meat

Serve the ground meat and lettuce leaves on separate dishes:
the guests then wrap their own packets.

SERVES 4

INGREDIENTS

1 cup ground pork or chicken
1 tbsp finely chopped Chinese mushrooms
1 tbsp finely chopped water chestnuts
pinch of sugar
1 tsp light soy sauce
1 tsp Chinese rice wine or dry sherry
1 tsp cornstarch
2–3 tbsp vegetable oil
½ tsp finely chopped ginger root
1 tsp finely chopped scallions
1 tbsp finely chopped Szechuan
preserved vegetables (optional)
1 tbsp oyster sauce
a few drops of sesame oil
salt and pepper
8 crisp lettuce leaves, to serve

1 Mix the ground meat with the mushrooms, water chestnuts, sugar, soy sauce, wine, cornstarch, and salt and pepper.

2 Heat the oil in a preheated wok or skillet and add the ginger and scallions, followed by the meat. Stir-fry for 1 minute.

3 Add the Szechuan preserved vegetables and continue stirring for 1 more minute. Add the oyster sauce and sesame oil, blend well, and cook for 1 more minute. Remove to a warm serving dish.

4 To serve: place about 2–3 tablespoons of the mixture on a lettuce leaf and roll it up tightly to form a small packet. Eat with your fingers.

Step *1*

Step *2*

Step *3*

Deep-Fried Shrimp

Use raw tiger shrimp in their shells. They are 3–4 inches long, and you should get 18–20 shrimp per 1 lb.

SERVES 4

INGREDIENTS

8–10 oz raw shrimp
in their shells, defrosted if frozen
1 tbsp light soy sauce
1 tsp Chinese rice wine or dry sherry
2 tsp cornstarch
vegetable oil, for deep-frying
2–3 scallions, to garnish

SPICY SALT AND PEPPER

1 tbsp salt
1 tsp ground Szechuan peppercorns
1 tsp five-spice powder

1 Pull the soft legs off the shrimp, but leave the body shell intact. Dry well on paper towels.

2 Place the shrimp in a bowl with the soy sauce, wine, and cornstarch. Turn to coat and leave to marinate for about 25–30 minutes.

3 To make the spicy salt and pepper, mix the salt, pepper, and five-spice powder together. Place in a dry skillet and stir-fry for about 3–4 minutes over a low heat, stirring constantly. Remove from the heat and allow to cool.

4 Heat the oil in a preheated wok until smoking, then deep-fry the shrimp in batches until golden brown. Remove with a slotted spoon and drain thoroughly on paper towels.

5 Place the scallions in a bowl, pour on 1 tablespoon of the hot oil, and leave for 30 seconds. Serve the shrimp garnished with the scallions, and with the spicy salt and pepper as a condiment.

Step *1*

Step *3*

Step *4*

Butterfly Shrimp

Use unpeeled, raw jumbo or tiger shrimp
which are about 3–4 inches long.

SERVES 4

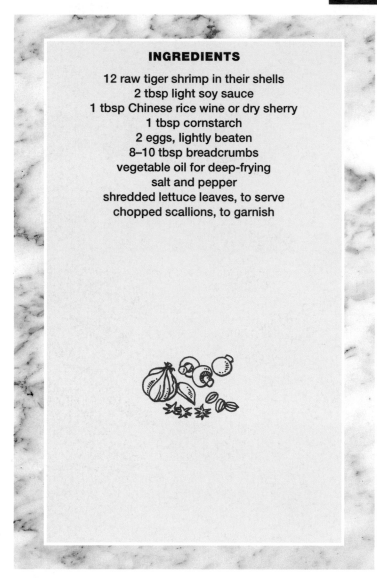

INGREDIENTS

12 raw tiger shrimp in their shells
2 tbsp light soy sauce
1 tbsp Chinese rice wine or dry sherry
1 tbsp cornstarch
2 eggs, lightly beaten
8–10 tbsp breadcrumbs
vegetable oil for deep-frying
salt and pepper
shredded lettuce leaves, to serve
chopped scallions, to garnish

1 Shell and devein the shrimp, but leave the tails on. Split them in half from the underbelly about halfway along, leaving the tails still firmly attached.

2 Mix together the soy sauce, wine, cornstarch, and salt and pepper in a bowl, add the shrimp, and turn to coat. Leave to marinate for 10–15 minutes.

3 Heat the oil in a preheated wok. Pick up each shrimp by the tail, dip it in the beaten egg, then roll it in the breadcrumbs to coat well.

4 Deep-fry the shrimp in batches until golden brown. Remove them with a slotted spoon and drain on paper towels.

5 To serve, arrange the shrimp neatly on a bed of lettuce leaves and garnish with scallions, either raw or soaked in a tablespoon of the hot oil for about 30 seconds.

Step *1*

Step *3*

Step *3*

Deep-Fried Sparerib

*The sparerib should be chopped into small, bite-size
pieces before or after cooking.*

SERVES 4

INGREDIENTS

8–10 finger ribs
1 tsp five-spice powder or
1 tbsp mild curry powder
1 tbsp rice wine or dry sherry
1 egg
2 tbsp all-purpose flour
vegetable oil for deep-frying
1 tsp finely shredded scallions
1 tsp finely shredded fresh green or
red hot chilies, deseeded
salt and pepper
Spicy Salt and Pepper (page 28), to serve

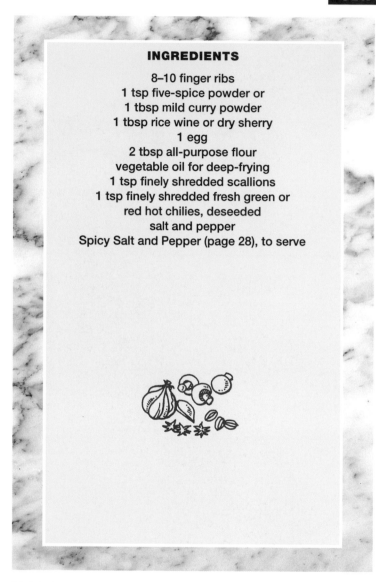

1 Chop the ribs into 3–4 small pieces. Place the ribs in a bowl with the five-spice or curry powder, wine, and salt and pepper. Turn to coat them, then leave to marinate for 1–2 hours.

2 Mix the egg and flour together to make a batter. Dip the ribs in the batter one by one to coat well.

3 Heat the oil in a preheated wok until smoking. Deep-fry the ribs for 4–5 minutes, then remove with a slotted spoon and drain on paper towels.

4 Reheat the oil over a high heat and deep-fry the ribs once more for another minute. Remove and drain again on paper towels.

5 Pour 1 tablespoon of the hot oil over the scallions and chilies and leave for 30–40 seconds. Serve the ribs with spicy salt and pepper, garnished with the shredded scallions and chilies.

Step *1*

Step *2*

Step *3*

Pork with Chili and Garlic Sauce

Any leftovers from this dish can be used for a number of other dishes, such as Hot & Sour Soup (page 60), and Twice-Cooked Pork (page 158).

SERVES 4

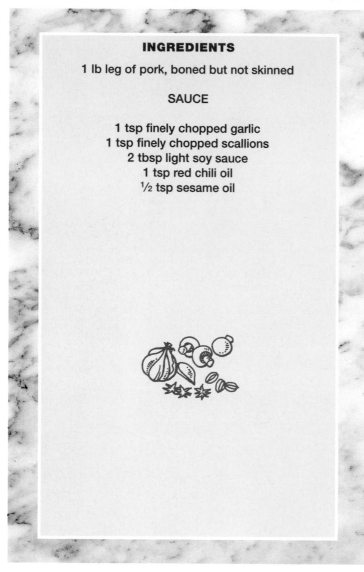

INGREDIENTS

1 lb leg of pork, boned but not skinned

SAUCE

1 tsp finely chopped garlic
1 tsp finely chopped scallions
2 tbsp light soy sauce
1 tsp red chili oil
½ tsp sesame oil

1 Place the pork, tied together in one piece, in a large pan, add enough cold water to cover, and bring to a rolling boil over a medium heat.

2 Skim off the scum that rises to the surface, cover, and simmer gently for 25–30 minutes.

3 Leave the meat in the liquid to cool, under cover, for at least 1–2 hours. Lift out the meat with 2 perforated spoons and leave to cool completely, skin-side up, for 2–3 hours.

4 To serve, cut off the skin, leaving a very thin layer of fat on top like a ham joint. Cut the meat in small, thin slices across the grain, and arrange neatly on a plate. Mix together the sauce ingredients, and pour the sauce evenly over the pork.

Step *2*

Step *3*

Step *4*

Barbecue Sparerib

This is a simplified version of the half saddle of pork ribs seen hanging in the windows of Cantonese restaurants. Use the specially small, thin ribs known as finger ribs.

SERVES 4

INGREDIENTS

1 lb finger ribs
1 tbsp sugar
1 tbsp light soy sauce
1 tbsp dark soy sauce
3 tbsp hoi-sin sauce
1 tbsp rice wine or dry sherry
4–5 tbsp water or Chinese Stock (page 16)
mild chili sauce, to dip
cilantro leaves, to garnish

1 Trim off any excess fat from the ribs and cut into pieces. Mix the ribs with the sugar, light and dark soy sauce, hoi-sin sauce, and wine in a baking dish, and marinate for about 2–3 hours.

2 Add the water or stock to the ribs and spread them out in the dish. Roast in a preheated oven, 425°F, for 15 minutes.

3 Turn the ribs over, lower the heat to 375°F, and cook for 30–35 minutes longer.

4 To serve, chop each rib into 3–4 small, bite-size pieces with a large knife or Chinese cleaver and arrange on a serving dish. Pour the sauce from the baking dish over them, garnish with cilantro leaves, and serve with chili sauce as a dip.

Step *2*

Step *3*

Step *4*

Barbecue Pork (Char Siu)

Also called honey-roasted pork, these are the strips of reddish meat
sometimes seen hanging in the windows of Cantonese restaurants.

SERVES 4

INGREDIENTS

1 lb pork tenderloin
⅔ cup boiling water
1 tbsp honey, dissolved in a little hot water
shredded lettuce, to serve

MARINADE

1 tbsp sugar
1 tbsp crushed yellow bean sauce
1 tbsp light soy sauce
1 tbsp hoi-sin sauce
1 tbsp oyster sauce
½ tsp chili sauce
1 tbsp brandy or rum
1 tsp sesame oil

1 Cut the pork into strips about 1 in. thick and 7–8 inches long and place in a large shallow dish. Combine the marinade ingredients and add to the pork, turning until well coated. Cover and leave to marinate for at least 3–4 hours, turning occasionally.

2 Remove the pork strips from the dish with a perforated spoon, reserving the marinade. Arrange the pork strips on a rack over a roasting pan. Place the pan in the preheated oven, 425°F, and pour in the boiling water. Roast for about 10–15 minutes.

3 Lower the oven temperature to 350°F. Baste the pork strips with the reserved marinade and turn. Roast for a further 10 minutes.

4 Remove the pork from the oven, brush with the honey syrup, and lightly brown under a medium hot broiler for 3–4 minutes, turning once or twice.

5 To serve, allow the pork to cool slightly before cutting it. Cut across the grain into thin slices and arrange on a bed of shredded lettuce. Make a sauce by boiling the marinade and the drippings in the roasting pan for a few minutes, strain, and pour over the pork.

Step *1*

Step *4*

Step *5*

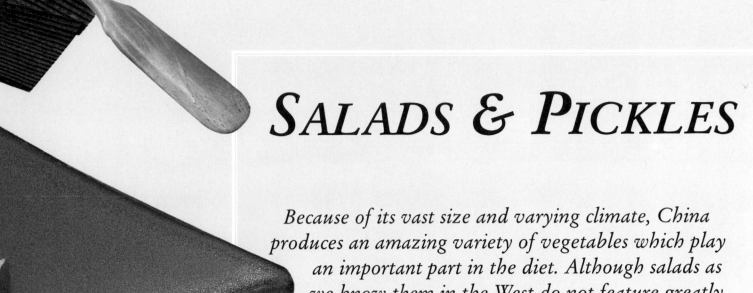

SALADS & PICKLES

Because of its vast size and varying climate, China produces an amazing variety of vegetables which play an important part in the diet. Although salads as we know them in the West do not feature greatly on the Chinese menu, many lightly-cooked vegetable dishes can be classified as salads when allowed to cool and lightly tossed with a dressing. Raw vegetables can be mixed with cooked ones to provide contrasting texture.

Dressings provide the necessary note of sharpness and acidity and can be based on palate-tingling mixtures of lime, fish sauce, ginger, soy sauce, and sesame oil, as well as the more familiar oil and vinegar.

For the Chinese, it is of the utmost importance to use the best, freshest vegetables available, preferably picked fresh as they are needed. Brief cooking and the necessary balance of texture and flavor, sweetness and acidity soon reveal inferior ingredients.

It is common practice in China to pickle vegetables for use in the winter months. These are used as a condiment, or stir-fried with vegetables or tofu, or added to soups. You can also make pickles with briefly marinated vegetables such as Sweet and Sour Cucumber (page 44) to use as salads.

Chinese Hot Salad

Stir-fried vegetables with a little touch of chili. To serve cold, add French dressing as the vegetables cool, toss well, and serve.

SERVES 4

INGREDIENTS

1 tbsp dark soy sauce
1½–2 tsp sweet chili sauce
2 tbsp sherry
1 tbsp brown sugar
1 tbsp wine vinegar
2 tbsp sunflower oil
1 garlic clove, crushed
4 scallions,
sliced thinly diagonally
8 oz zucchini cut into
julienne strips about 1½ inches long
8 oz carrots, cut into julienne strips
about 1½ inches long
1 red or green bell pepper,
cored, deseeded, and sliced thinly
14 oz can bean-sprouts, well drained
4 oz green or fine beans,
cut into 2 in. lengths
1 tbsp sesame oil
salt and pepper
1–2 tsp sesame seeds, to garnish

1 Blend the soy sauce, chili sauce, sherry, sugar, vinegar, and salt and pepper together.

2 Heat the 2 tablespoons of sunflower oil in a wok, swirling it around until it is really hot.

3 Add the garlic and scallions to the wok and stir-fry for 1–2 minutes.

4 Add the zucchini, carrots, and bell pepper and stir-fry for 1–2 minutes, then add the soy sauce mixture, and bring to a boil.

5 Add the bean-sprouts and green beans and stir-fry for 1–2 minutes, making sure all the vegetables are thoroughly coated with the sauce.

6 Drizzle the sesame oil over the vegetables. Stir–fry for about 30 seconds and sprinkle with sesame seeds.

Step *1*

Step *4*

Step *5*

Sweet & Sour Cucumber

Chunks of cucumber are marinated in vinegar and sweetened
with honey to make a sweet and sour salad.

SERVES 4

INGREDIENTS

1 cucumber
1 tsp salt
2 tsp honey
2 tbsp rice vinegar
3 tbsp chopped fresh cilantro
2 tsp sesame oil
¼ tsp crushed red peppercorns
strips of red and yellow bell pepper, to garnish

1 Peel thin strips off the cucumber along the length. This gives a pretty striped effect. Cut the cucumber in fourths lengthwise, and then into 1 in. long pieces. Place in a colander.

2 Sprinkle the salt over the cucumber and leave for 30 minutes to allow the salt to draw out excess water. Wash the cucumber thoroughly to remove the salt, drain, and pat dry with paper towels.

3 Place the cucumber in a bowl. Combine the honey with the vinegar and pour over. Mix together and leave to marinate for 15 minutes.

4 Stir in the cilantro and sesame oil, and place in a serving bowl.

5 Sprinkle over the crushed red peppercorns. Serve garnished with strips of red and yellow bell pepper.

Step *1*

Step *2*

Step *4*

Sweet & Sour Tofu Salad

Tofu mixed with crisp stir-fried vegetables, then tossed in a piquant sweet and sour dressing makes an ideal light meal or starter.

SERVES 4–6

INGREDIENTS

2 tbsp vegetable oil
1 tbsp sesame oil
1 garlic clove, crushed
1 lb tofu, cubed
1 onion, sliced
1 carrot, cut into julienne strips
1 celery stalk, sliced
2 small red bell peppers,
cored, deseeded, and sliced
8 oz snow peas,
trimmed and halved
4 oz broccoli,
trimmed and divided into flowerets
4 oz thin green beans, halved
2 tbsp oyster sauce
1 tbsp tamarind concentrate
1 tbsp fish sauce
1 tbsp tomato paste
1 tbsp light soy sauce
1 tbsp chili sauce
2 tbsp sugar
1 tbsp white vinegar
pinch of ground star anise
1 tsp cornstarch
1¼ cups water

1 Heat the vegetable oil in a wok or large, heavy-based skillet until hot. Add the crushed garlic and cook for a few seconds.

2 Add the tofu in batches and stir-fry over a gentle heat, until golden on all sides. Remove with a slotted spoon and keep warm.

3 Add the onion, carrot, celery, red bell pepper, snow peas, broccoli, and green beans to the wok or skillet and stir-fry for about 2–3 minutes or until tender-crisp.

4 Add the oyster sauce, tamarind concentrate, fish sauce, tomato paste, soy sauce, chili sauce, sugar, vinegar, and star anise, mixing well to blend. Stir-fry for a further 2 minutes.

5 Mix the cornstarch with the water and add to the pan with the fried tofu. Stir-fry gently until the sauce boils and thickens slightly.

6 Serve the salad immediately, on warm plates.

Step *2*

Step *3*

Step *5*

Oriental Salad

*This colorful crisp salad has a fresh orange dressing
and is topped with crunchy vermicelli.*

SERVES 4–6

INGREDIENTS

¼ cup dried vermicelli
½ head Chinese leaves
2 cups bean-sprouts
6 radishes
4 oz snow peas
1 large carrot
4 oz sprouting beans

DRESSING

juice of 1 orange
1 tbsp sesame seeds, toasted
1 tsp honey
1 tsp sesame oil
1 tbsp hazelnut oil

1 Break the vermicelli into small strands. Heat a wok or skillet and dry-fry the vermicelli until lightly golden. Remove from the wok or skillet and set aside.

2 Shred the Chinese leaves and wash with the bean-sprouts. Drain thoroughly and place in a large bowl. Slice the radishes. Trim the snow peas and cut each into 3. Cut the carrot into thin matchsticks. Add the sprouting beans and prepared vegetables to the bowl.

3 Place all the dressing ingredients in a screw-top jar and shake until well-blended. Pour over the salad and toss.

4 Transfer the salad to a serving bowl and sprinkle over the reserved vermicelli before serving.

Step *1*

Step *2*

Step *4*

Pickled Vegetables

Pickled vegetables can be marinated for as little as 30 minutes or for several days.

SERVES 4

INGREDIENTS

PICKLED CUCUMBER

1 cucumber, about 12 inches long
1 tsp salt
2 tsp superfine sugar
1 tsp rice vinegar
1 tsp red chili oil
a few drops of sesame oil

MIXED PICKLED VEGETABLES

12 oz Chinese leaves,
cut into bite-size pieces
2 oz green beans, topped and tailed
4 oz carrots, diced
3 chilies, deseeded and chopped finely
2 tsp Szechuan peppercorns
2 tbsp coarse salt
2 tbsp rice wine

PICKLED CUCUMBER

1 Halve the cucumber, unpeeled, lengthwise. Scrape off the seeds and cut across into thick chunks.

2 Sprinkle with the salt and mix well. Leave for at least 20–30 minutes, longer if possible, then pour all of the juice away.

3 Mix the cucumber with the sugar, vinegar, and chili oil, and lightly sprinkle with the sesame oil just before serving.

MIXED PICKLED VEGETABLES

1 Place the vegetables in a glass bowl with the chilies, peppercorns, salt, and wine. Stir well, cover, and leave to marinate in the refrigerator for 4 days. Serve cold, as a salad.

Step *1*

Step *2*

Step *3*

Hot & Sour Duck Salad

This is a lovely tangy salad, drizzled with a lime juice and fish sauce dressing. It makes a splendid starter or light main course dish.

SERVES 4

INGREDIENTS

2 heads crisp salad lettuce,
washed and separated into leaves
2 shallots, sliced thinly
4 scallions, chopped
1 celery stalk, cut into julienne strips
2-in. piece cucumber,
cut into julienne strips
4 oz bean-sprouts
7 oz can water chestnuts,
drained and sliced
4 duck breast fillets, roasted and sliced
orange slices, to serve

DRESSING

3 tbsp fish sauce
1½ tbsp lime juice
2 garlic cloves, crushed
1 red chili, deseeded and
chopped very finely
1 green chili, deseeded and
chopped very finely
1 tsp palm sugar or demerara sugar

1 Mix the lettuce leaves with the shallots, scallions, celery, cucumber, bean-sprouts, and water chestnuts. Place the mixture on a large serving platter.

2 Arrange the duck breast slices on top of the salad in an attractive overlapping pattern.

3 To make the dressing, put the fish sauce, lime juice, garlic, chilies, and sugar into a small pan. Heat gently, stirring constantly. Taste and adjust the piquancy if liked by adding more lime juice, or add more fish sauce to reduce the sharpness.

4 Drizzle the warm salad dressing over the duck salad and serve immediately.

Step *1*

Step *2*

Step *3*

SOUPS

Soup is not normally served as a separate course in China, except at formal occasions and banquets - and then it usually appears toward the end of the meal. At an everyday meal in Chinese homes it is quite common to have a large tureen of soup on the table which is served at the same time as the other dishes. The soup is almost always a clear broth in which a small amount of thinly sliced vegetables and/or meat have been quickly poached.

Although most Chinese soups are of the thin, clear variety, they do have a few thickened ones, such as Hot & Sour Soup (page 60) to which cornstarch is added. These soups can be eaten as a lunch or snack on their own.

The soup should ideally be made with a good stock. If this is unavailable, a Chinese cook would simply stir-fry the ingredients first in a little oil, then add water and seasonings (salt, soy sauce, or monosodium glutamate) to make an instant soup fit for the gods! If you use a stock cube, remember to reduce the amount of seasonings in the recipe as most commercially-made bouillon cubes are fairly salty. It is always worth making your own Chinese stock (page 16) if you have time.

Mushroom & Cucumber Noodle Soup

A light, refreshing clear soup of mushrooms, cucumber, and small pieces of rice noodles, flavored with soy sauce and a touch of garlic.

SERVES 4

INGREDIENTS

4 oz flat or open-cup mushrooms
½ cucumber
2 scallions
1 garlic clove
2 tbsp vegetable oil
¼ cup Chinese rice sticks
¾ tsp salt
1 tbsp soy sauce

1 Wash the mushrooms and slice thinly. Do not remove the peel as this adds more flavor. Halve the cucumber lengthwise. Scoop out the seeds, using a teaspoon, and slice the cucumber thinly.

2 Chop the scallions finely and cut the garlic clove into thin strips.

3 Heat the oil in a wok or large saucepan. Add the scallions and garlic, and stir-fry for 30 seconds. Add the mushrooms and stir-fry for 2–3 minutes.

4 Stir in 2½ cups water. Break the noodles into short lengths and add them to the soup. Bring to a boil.

5 Add the cucumber slices, salt, and soy sauce, and simmer for 2–3 minutes.

6 Serve the soup in warm bowls, distributing the noodles and vegetables evenly.

Step *1*

Step *3*

Step *5*

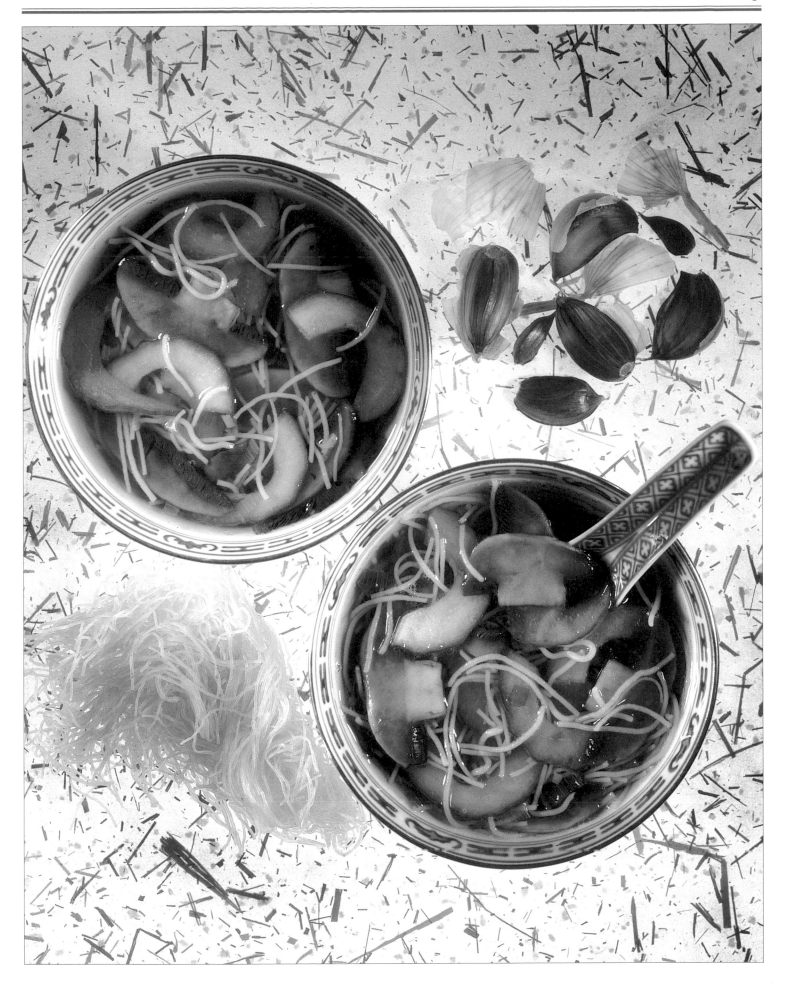

Mixed Vegetable Soup

*Select three or four vegetables for this soup: the Chinese like to blend
different colors, flavors, and textures to create harmony as well as contrast.*

SERVES 4

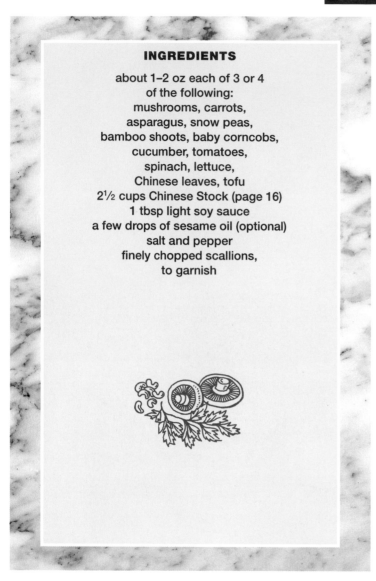

INGREDIENTS

about 1–2 oz each of 3 or 4
of the following:
mushrooms, carrots,
asparagus, snow peas,
bamboo shoots, baby corncobs,
cucumber, tomatoes,
spinach, lettuce,
Chinese leaves, tofu
2½ cups Chinese Stock (page 16)
1 tbsp light soy sauce
a few drops of sesame oil (optional)
salt and pepper
finely chopped scallions,
to garnish

1 Cut your selection of vegetables into roughly uniform shapes and sizes (slices, shreds, or cubes).

2 Bring the stock to a rolling boil in a wok and add the vegetables, bearing in mind that some require a longer cooking time than others: add carrots and baby corncobs first, cook for 2 minutes, then add asparagus, mushrooms, Chinese leaves, tofu, and cook for another minute.

3 Add the spinach, lettuce, watercress, cucumber, and tomato. Stir, and bring the soup back to a boil.

4 Add soy sauce and the sesame oil, and adjust the seasoning. Serve hot, garnished with scallions.

Step *1*

Step *3*

Step *4*

Hot & Sour Soup

This is the favorite soup in Chinese restaurants throughout the world.

SERVES 4

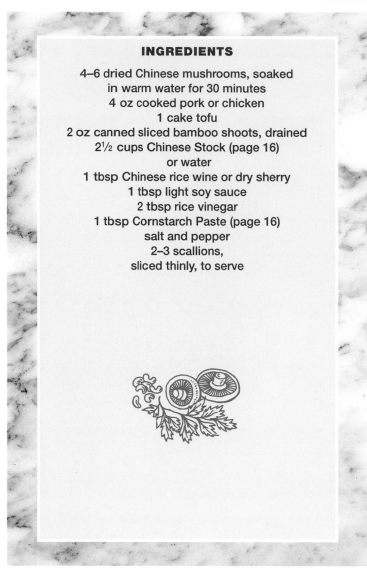

INGREDIENTS

4–6 dried Chinese mushrooms, soaked
in warm water for 30 minutes
4 oz cooked pork or chicken
1 cake tofu
2 oz canned sliced bamboo shoots, drained
2½ cups Chinese Stock (page 16)
or water
1 tbsp Chinese rice wine or dry sherry
1 tbsp light soy sauce
2 tbsp rice vinegar
1 tbsp Cornstarch Paste (page 16)
salt and pepper
2–3 scallions,
sliced thinly, to serve

1 Drain the mushrooms, squeeze dry, and discard the hard stems. Thinly slice the mushrooms.

2 Thinly slice the meat, tofu, and bamboo shoots into narrow shreds.

3 Bring the stock or water to a rolling boil in a wok or large pan and add all the ingredients. Bring back to a boil, then simmer for about 1 minute.

4 Add the wine, soy sauce, vinegar, and salt and pepper.

5 Bring back to a boil once more, stirring in the cornstarch paste to thicken the soup. Serve hot, sprinkled with the scallions.

Step *1*

Step *2*

Step *5*

Vegetarian Hot & Sour Soup

*This is a popular Chinese soup, which is unusual in that it is thickened.
The 'hot' flavor is achieved by the addition of plenty of black pepper.*

SERVES 4

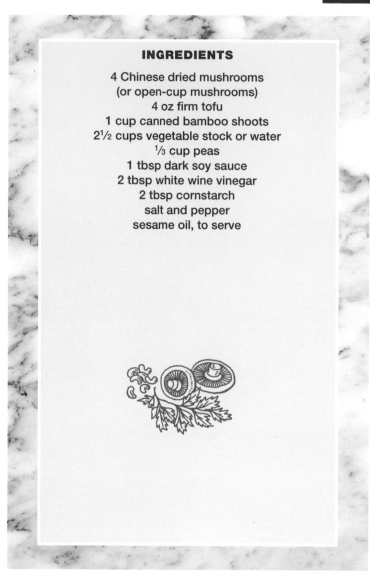

INGREDIENTS

4 Chinese dried mushrooms
(or open-cup mushrooms)
4 oz firm tofu
1 cup canned bamboo shoots
2½ cups vegetable stock or water
⅓ cup peas
1 tbsp dark soy sauce
2 tbsp white wine vinegar
2 tbsp cornstarch
salt and pepper
sesame oil, to serve

1 Place the dried mushrooms in a bowl and cover with warm water. Leave to soak for 20–25 minutes.

2 Drain the mushrooms and squeeze out the excess water, reserving this. Remove the tough centers and cut the mushrooms into thin shreds. Shred the tofu and bamboo shoots.

3 Bring the stock or water to a boil in a large saucepan. Add the mushrooms, tofu, bamboo shoots, and peas. Simmer for 2 minutes.

4 Mix together the soy sauce, vinegar, and cornstarch with 2 tablespoons of the reserved mushroom liquid. Stir into the soup with the remaining mushroom liquid. Bring to a boil and season with salt and plenty of pepper. Simmer for 2 minutes.

5 Serve in warm bowls with a few drops of sesame oil in each.

Step 2

Step 3

Step 4

Wonton Soup

Filled wontons are served in a clear soup. The recipe for the wonton skins makes 24 but the soup requires only 12 – freeze the rest for another time.

SERVES 4

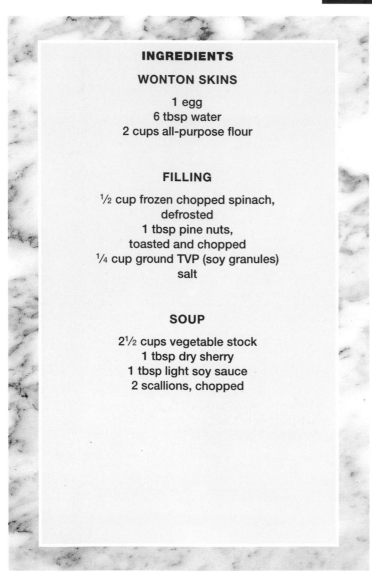

INGREDIENTS

WONTON SKINS

1 egg
6 tbsp water
2 cups all-purpose flour

FILLING

½ cup frozen chopped spinach, defrosted
1 tbsp pine nuts, toasted and chopped
¼ cup ground TVP (soy granules)
salt

SOUP

2½ cups vegetable stock
1 tbsp dry sherry
1 tbsp light soy sauce
2 scallions, chopped

1 Beat the egg lightly in a bowl and mix with the water. Stir in the flour to form a stiff dough. Knead lightly, then cover with a damp cloth, and leave to rest for 30 minutes.

2 Roll the dough out into a large sheet about ¼ in. thick. Cut out 3 in. squares. Dust each one lightly with flour. Only 12 squares are required for the soup so freeze the remainder.

3 To make the filling, squeeze out the excess water from the spinach. Mix the spinach with the pine nuts and TVP (soy granules). Season with salt.

4 Divide the mixture into 12 equal portions and place one portion in the center of each square. Seal by bringing the opposite corners of each square together and squeezing well.

5 To make the soup, bring the stock, sherry, and soy sauce to a boil, add the wontons, and boil rapidly for 2–3 minutes. Add the scallions and serve in warm bowls immediately

Step 2

Step 4

Step 5

Spinach & Tofu Soup

This is a very colorful and delicious soup. If spinach is not in season,
watercress or lettuce can be used instead.

SERVES 4

INGREDIENTS

1 cake tofu
4 oz spinach leaves without stems
3 cups Chinese Stock (page 16)
or water
1 tbsp light soy sauce
salt and pepper

1 Cut the tofu into small pieces about ¼ in. thick. Wash the spinach leaves and cut them into small pieces or shreds, discarding any discolored leaves and tough stalks. (If possible, use fresh young spinach leaves, which have not yet developed tough ribs. Otherwise, it is important to cut out all the ribs and stems for this soup.)

2 In a wok or large pan, bring the stock to a rolling boil. Add the tofu and soy sauce, bring back to a boil, and simmer for about 2 minutes over a medium heat.

3 Add the spinach and simmer for 1 more minute.

4 Skim the surface of the soup to make it clear, adjust the seasoning, and serve.

Step *1*

Step *2*

Step *3*

Seafood & Tofu Soup

Use shrimp, squid, or scallops,
or a combination of all three.

SERVES 4

INGREDIENTS

8 oz seafood, such as peeled shrimp,
squid, scallops, defrosted if frozen
½ egg white, beaten lightly
1 tbsp Cornstarch Paste (page 16)
1 cake tofu
3 cups Chinese Stock (page 16)
1 tbsp light soy sauce
salt and pepper
fresh cilantro leaves, to garnish (optional)

1 Small shrimp can be left whole; larger ones should be cut into smaller pieces. Cut the squid and scallops into small pieces.

2 If raw, mix the shrimp and scallops with the egg white and cornstarch paste to prevent them from becoming tough when they are cooked.

3 Cut the tofu into about 24 small cubes.

4 Bring the stock to a rolling boil. Add the tofu and soy sauce, bring back to a boil, and simmer for 1 minute.

5 Stir in the seafood, raw pieces first, pre-cooked ones last. Bring back to a boil and simmer for just 1 minute. Adjust the seasoning and serve garnished with cilantro leaves, if liked.

Step 1

Step 2

Step 5

Fish & Vegetable Soup

A chunky fish soup with strips of vegetables,
flavored with ginger and lemon, makes a meal in itself.

SERVES 4

INGREDIENTS

8 oz white fish fillets, such as
cod, halibut, haddock, sole
½ tsp ground ginger
½ tsp salt
1 small leek, trimmed and sliced
1 tbsp sunflower oil
1 large carrot, cut into julienne strips
8 canned water chestnuts, sliced thinly
5 cups fish or vegetable stock
1 tbsp lemon juice
1 tbsp light soy sauce
1 large zucchini,
cut into julienne strips
2–4 crab sticks (optional), defrosted if frozen
pepper

1 Remove any skin from the fish and cut the fish into cubes, about 1 in. Combine the ground ginger and salt and rub into the fish. Leave to marinate for at least 30 minutes.

2 Meanwhile, divide the green and white parts of the leek. Cut each part into 1 in. lengths and then into julienne strips down the length of each piece, keeping the two parts separate. Slice the crab sticks into ½ in. pieces.

3 Heat the oil in the wok, swirling it around so it is really hot. Add the white part of the leek and stir-fry for a couple of minutes, then add the carrots and water chestnuts, and continue to cook for 1–2 minutes, stirring thoroughly.

4 Add the stock and bring to a boil, then add the lemon juice and soy sauce, and simmer for 2 minutes.

5 Add the fish and continue to cook for about 5 minutes until the fish begins to break up a little, then add the green part of the leek and the zucchini, and simmer for about 1 minute. Add the sliced crab sticks, if using, and season to taste with pepper. Simmer for a further minute or so and serve piping hot.

Step *1*

Step *2*

Step *5*

Three-Flavor Soup

*Ideally, use raw shrimp in this soup. If that is not possible,
add ready-cooked ones at the very last stage.*

SERVES 4

INGREDIENTS

4 oz boned and skinned chicken breast
4 oz raw peeled shrimp
salt
½ egg white, beaten lightly
2 tsp Cornstarch Paste (page 16)
4 oz honey-roast ham
3 cups Chinese Stock (page 16)
or water
finely chopped scallions,
to garnish

1 Thinly slice the chicken into small shreds. If the shrimp are large, cut each in half lengthwise, otherwise leave whole.

2 Place the chicken and shrimp in a bowl and mix with a pinch of salt, the egg white, and cornstarch paste until well coated.

3 Cut the ham into small thin slices roughly the same size as the chicken pieces.

4 Bring the stock or water to a rolling boil, add the chicken, the raw shrimp, and the ham. Bring the soup back to a boil, and simmer for 1 minute.

5 Adjust the seasoning and serve the soup hot, garnished with the scallions.

Step *2*

Step *3*

Step *4*

Shrimp Soup

A mixture of textures and flavors makes this an interesting and colorful soup. The egg may be made into a flat omelet and added as thin strips.

SERVES 4

INGREDIENTS

2 tbsp sunflower oil
2 scallions,
sliced thinly diagonally
1 carrot, grated coarsely
4 oz large closed cup mushrooms,
sliced thinly
4 cups fish or vegetable stock
½ tsp Chinese five-spice powder
1 tbsp light soy sauce
4 oz large peeled shrimp or peeled tiger shrimp,
defrosted if frozen
½ bunch of watercress,
trimmed and chopped roughly
1 egg, beaten well
salt and pepper
4 large shrimp in shells,
to garnish (optional)

1 Heat the oil in a wok, swirling it around until really hot. Add the scallions and stir-fry for a minute, then add the carrots and mushrooms, and continue to cook for about 2 minutes.

2 Add the stock and bring to a boil, then season to taste with salt and pepper, five-spice powder, and soy sauce. Simmer for 5 minutes.

3 If the shrimp are really large, cut them in half before adding to the wok, then continue to simmer for 3–4 minutes.

4 Add the roughly chopped watercress to the wok and mix well, then slowly pour in the beaten egg in a circular movement so that it cooks in threads in the soup.

5 Adjust the seasoning and serve each portion topped with a whole shrimp.

Step *1*

Step *2*

Step *4*

Corn & Crab Meat Soup

You must use creamed corn for this soup since it originated in the United States. Chicken can be used instead of the crab meat.

SERVES 4

INGREDIENTS:

4 oz crab meat, or
cooked chicken breast
¼ tsp finely chopped ginger root
2 egg whites
2 tbsp milk
1 tbsp Cornstarch Paste (page 16)
2½ cups Chinese Stock (page 16)
7 oz can creamed corn
salt and pepper
finely chopped scallions,
to garnish

1 Flake the crab meat (or coarsely chop the chicken breast) and mix with the ginger.

2 Beat the egg whites until frothy, add the milk and cornstarch paste, and beat again until smooth. Blend in the crab or chicken.

3 In a wok or large skillet, bring the stock to a boil, add the creamed corn, and bring back to a boil.

4 Stir in the crab meat or chicken pieces and egg-white mixture, adjust the seasoning, and stir gently until the mixture is well blended. Serve hot, garnished with chopped scallions.

Step 2

Step 3

Step 4

Chicken & Corn Soup

*A hint of chili and sherry flavor this chicken and corn soup which
contains red bell pepper and tomato for color and flavor.*

SERVES 4

INGREDIENTS

1 boned and skinned chicken breast,
about 6 oz
2 tbsp sunflower oil
2–3 scallions,
thinly sliced diagonally
1 small or ½ large red bell pepper,
cored, deseeded, and sliced thinly
1 garlic clove, crushed
4 oz baby corncobs, sliced thinly
4 cups chicken stock
7 oz can corn kernels, well drained
2 tbsp sherry
2–3 tsp bottled sweet chili sauce
2–3 tsp cornstarch
2 tomatoes, skinned, quartered, and deseeded,
then sliced
salt and pepper
freshly chopped cilantro
or parsley, to garnish

1 Cut the chicken breast into 4 strips lengthwise, then
cut each strip into narrow slices across the grain.

2 Heat the oil in a wok, swirling it around until it is
really hot. Add the chicken and stir-fry for 3–4
minutes, spreading it out over the wok until it is well
sealed all over and almost cooked.

3 Add the scallions, bell pepper, and garlic and
continue to stir-fry for 2–3 minutes, then add the
baby corncobs and stock, and bring to a boil.

4 Add the corn kernels, sherry, and sweet chili sauce
and salt to taste and simmer for 5 minutes, stirring
from time to time.

5 Blend the cornstarch with a little cold water, add to
the soup, and bring to a boil. Add the strips of
tomato, adjust the seasoning, and simmer for a few
minutes. Serve the soup very hot, sprinkled with finely
chopped cilantro or parsley.

Step *2*

Step *3*

Step *4*

Chicken Soup with Almonds

This soup can also be made using turkey or pheasant breasts.
Pheasant gives a stronger, gamy flavor.

SERVES 4

INGREDIENTS

1 large or 2 small boned and skinned
chicken breasts
1 tbsp sunflower oil
4 scallions,
thinly sliced diagonally
1 carrot, cut into julienne strips
3 cups chicken stock
finely grated rind of ½ lemon
⅓ cup ground almonds
1 tbsp light soy sauce
1 tbsp lemon juice
¼ cup slivered
almonds, toasted
salt and pepper

1 Cut each breast into 4 strips lengthwise, then slice very thinly across the grain to give shreds of chicken.

2 Heat the oil in the wok, swirling it around until really hot. Add the chicken and toss for 3–4 minutes until sealed and almost cooked through. Then add the carrot and continue to cook for 2–3 minutes, stirring all the time. Add the scallions and stir.

3 Add the stock to the wok and bring to a boil. Add the lemon rind, ground almonds, soy sauce, lemon juice, and plenty of seasoning. Bring back to a boil and simmer, uncovered, for 5 minutes, stirring occasionally.

4 Add most of the toasted slivered almonds and continue to cook for a further 1–2 minutes. Check the seasoning.

5 Serve the soup very hot, in individual bowls, sprinkled with the remaining almonds.

Step *1*

Step *2*

Step *3*

Noodles in Soup

*Noodles in soup (tang mein) are more popular than fried noodles (chow mein)
in China. You can use different ingredients for the dressing if preferred.*

SERVES 4

INGREDIENTS

8 oz boneless chicken breast, pork tenderloin,
or any other cooked meat
3–4 Chinese dried mushrooms, soaked
in warm water for 30 minutes
4 oz canned sliced bamboo shoots,
rinsed and drained
4 oz spinach leaves, lettuce hearts,
or Chinese leaves, shredded
2 scallions, shredded finely
8 oz egg noodles
about 2½ cups Chinese Stock (page 16)
2 tbsp light soy sauce
2 tbsp vegetable oil
1 tsp salt
½ tsp sugar
2 tsp Chinese rice wine or dry sherry
a few drops of sesame oil
1 tsp red chili oil (optional)

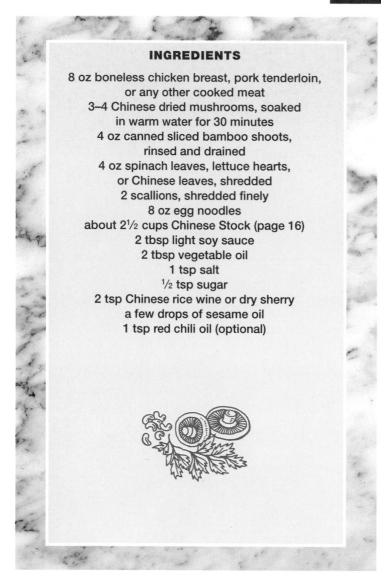

1 Cut the meat into thin shreds. Squeeze dry the soaked mushrooms and discard the hard stem.

2 Thinly shred the mushrooms, bamboo shoots, spinach leaves, and scallions.

3 Cook the noodles in boiling water according to the instructions on the packet, then drain, and rinse under cold water. Place in a bowl. Bring the stock to a boil, add about 1 tablespoon soy sauce, and pour over the noodles. Keep warm.

4 Heat the oil in a preheated wok, add the meat, vegetables, and about half of the scallions. Stir-fry for about 2–3 minutes. Add the salt, sugar, wine, sesame oil, and chili oil, if using.

5 Pour the mixture in the wok over the noodles, garnish with the remaining scallions, and serve immediately.

Step *2*

Step *4*

Step *5*

Pork & Szechuan Vegetable Soup

*Sold in cans, Szechuan preserved vegetable is pickled mustard root which
is quite hot and salty, so rinse in water before use.*

SERVES 4

INGREDIENTS

8 oz pork tenderloin
2 tsp Cornstarch Paste (page 16)
4 oz Szechuan preserved vegetable
3 cups Chinese Stock (page 16)
or water
salt and pepper
a few drops of sesame oil (optional)
2–3 scallions, sliced,
to garnish

1 Cut the pork across the grain into thin shreds and mix with the cornstarch paste.

2 Wash and rinse the Szechuan preserved vegetable, then cut into thin shreds the same size as the pork.

3 Bring the stock or water to a rolling boil, add the pork, and stir to separate the shreds. Bring back to a boil.

4 Add the Szechuan preserved vegetable and bring back to a boil once more. Adjust the seasoning and sprinkle with sesame oil. Serve hot, garnished with the scallion slices.

Step *1*

Step *2*

Step *4*

FISH & SEAFOOD

China's many miles of coastline, rivers, and lakes offer an enormous variety of fresh and salt-water fish and seafood. Among the most popular varieties are carp, bass, bream, Mandarin fish (a type of perch), shad, grouper, and sole. Seafood, such as clams, crab, crawfish, shrimp, and lobsters, are also widely eaten, and fresh-water crabs with their soft shells, are considered a great delicacy. Dishes which include shark's fins, abalone, squid, and edible seaweed are also common. Although fish and seafood are widely eaten in China, the Chinese do not like fishy smells. Ginger, garlic, and salty black bean sauce are often used to disguise such smells. Favorite cooking methods are steaming and quick poaching in boiling water or broth. Lobster and crabs are sometimes fried at very high temperatures in a flavored oil which penetrates the cracked shells and creates the most delectable sauce which the Chinese love to suck from the shells. The process of buying and cooking fish is taken very seriously in China, as it is a highly esteemed food. No cook with any pride would dream of buying anything but live fish, which are purchased in leakproof water-filled baskets and kept alive until just before cooking.

Stir-Fried Shrimp & Vegetables

This colorful and delicious dish is cooked with vegetables.
Vary them according to seasonal availability.

SERVES 4

INGREDIENTS

2 oz snow peas
½ small carrot, sliced thinly lengthwise
2 oz baby corncobs
2 oz straw mushrooms
6–8 oz raw tiger shrimp, peeled
1 tsp salt
½ egg white, beaten lightly
1 tsp Cornstarch Paste (page 16)
about 1¼ cups vegetable oil
1 scallion, cut into short sections
4 slices ginger root, chopped finely
½ tsp sugar
1 tbsp light soy sauce
1 tsp Chinese rice wine or dry sherry
a few drops of sesame oil

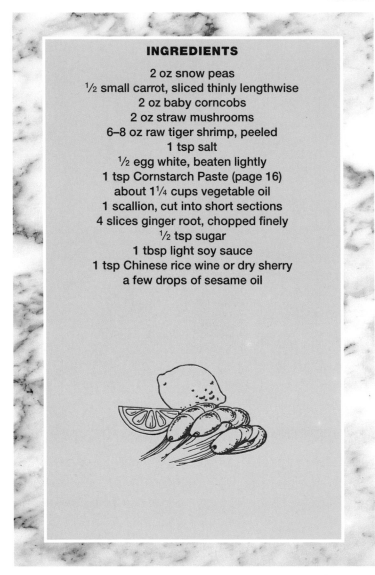

1 Top and tail the snow peas. Cut the carrot into the same size as the snow peas. Halve the baby corncobs and straw mushrooms.

2 Mix the shrimp with a pinch of the salt, the egg white, and cornstarch paste.

3 Heat a wok over high heat for 2–3 minutes, then add the oil, and heat to medium-hot. Add the shrimp, stirring to separate them. Remove with a perforated spoon as soon as the color changes.

4 Pour off the oil, leaving about 1 tablespoon in the wok. Add the snow peas, carrot, corncobs, mushrooms, scallion, and ginger root. Stir-fry for about 1 minute.

5 Add the shrimp and the sugar, soy sauce, and rice wine. Blend well. Sprinkle with the sesame oil and serve hot.

Step *1*

Step *3*

Step *5*

Stir-Fried Shrimp

*The green bell peppers in this dish can be replaced by either
snow peas or broccoli.*

SERVES 4

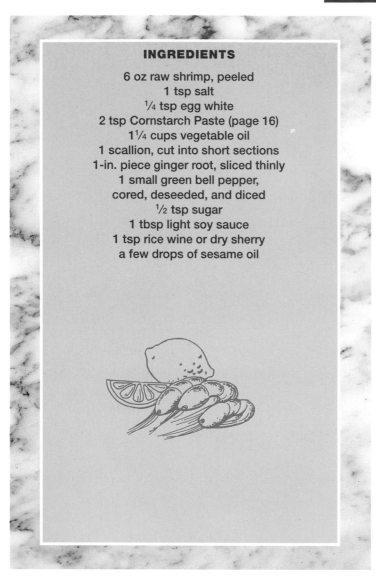

INGREDIENTS

6 oz raw shrimp, peeled
1 tsp salt
¼ tsp egg white
2 tsp Cornstarch Paste (page 16)
1¼ cups vegetable oil
1 scallion, cut into short sections
1-in. piece ginger root, sliced thinly
1 small green bell pepper,
cored, deseeded, and diced
½ tsp sugar
1 tbsp light soy sauce
1 tsp rice wine or dry sherry
a few drops of sesame oil

1 Mix the shrimp with a pinch of the salt, the egg white, and cornstarch paste until they are all well coated.

2 Heat the oil in a preheated wok and stir-fry the shrimp for 30–40 seconds only. Remove and drain on paper towels.

3 Pour off the oil, leaving about 1 tablespoon in the wok. Add the scallion and ginger to flavor the oil for a few seconds, then add the green bell pepper, and stir-fry for about 1 minute.

4 Add the remaining salt and the sugar, followed by the shrimp. Continue stirring for another minute or so, then add the soy sauce and wine, and blend well. Sprinkle with sesame oil and serve immediately.

Step *2*

Step *3*

Step *4*

Szechuan Shrimp

*Use raw shrimp if possible, otherwise omit steps 1
and 2, and add the cooked shrimp before the sauce at step 3.*

SERVES 4

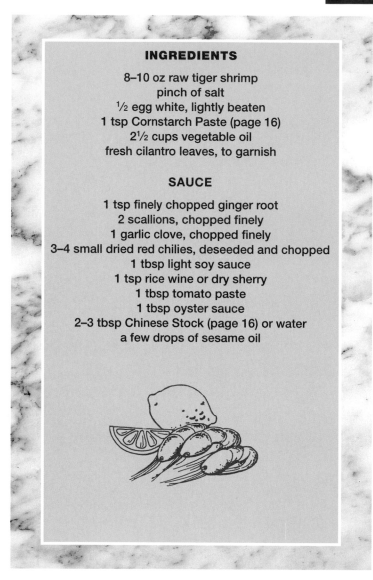

INGREDIENTS

8–10 oz raw tiger shrimp
pinch of salt
½ egg white, lightly beaten
1 tsp Cornstarch Paste (page 16)
2½ cups vegetable oil
fresh cilantro leaves, to garnish

SAUCE

1 tsp finely chopped ginger root
2 scallions, chopped finely
1 garlic clove, chopped finely
3–4 small dried red chilies, deseeded and chopped
1 tbsp light soy sauce
1 tsp rice wine or dry sherry
1 tbsp tomato paste
1 tbsp oyster sauce
2–3 tbsp Chinese Stock (page 16) or water
a few drops of sesame oil

1 Peel the raw shrimp, then mix with the salt, egg white, and cornstarch paste until well coated.

2 Heat the oil in a preheated wok until it is smoking, then deep-fry the shrimp in hot oil for about 1 minute. Remove with a perforated spoon and drain on paper towels.

3 Pour off the oil, leaving about 1 tablespoon in the wok. Add all the ingredients for the sauce, bring to a boil, and stir until smooth and well blended.

4 Add the shrimp to the sauce, stirring to blend. Garnish with cilantro leaves.

Step *1*

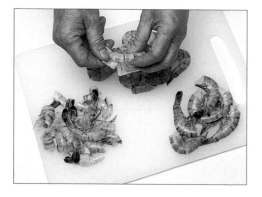

Step *3*

Step *4*

Sizzled Chili Shrimp

Large shrimp are marinated in a chili mixture then
stir-fried with cashews. Serve with fluffy rice and braised vegetables.

SERVES 4

INGREDIENTS

5 tbsp soy sauce
5 tbsp dry sherry
3 dried red chilies, deseeded and chopped
2 garlic cloves, crushed
2 tsp grated ginger root
5 tbsp water
1¼ lb shelled tiger shrimp
1 large bunch scallions, chopped
¾ cup salted cashew nuts
3 tbsp vegetable oil
2 tsp cornstarch

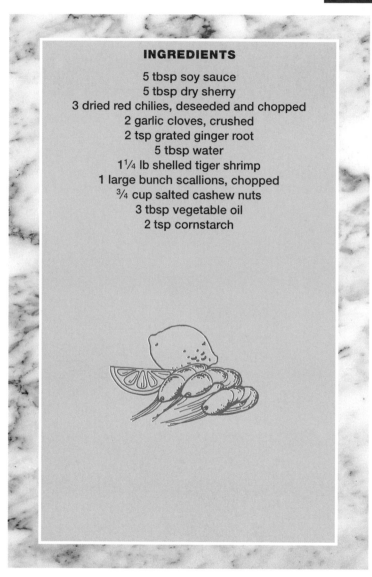

1 Mix the soy sauce with the sherry, chilies, garlic, ginger, and water in a large bowl.

2 Add the shrimp, scallions, and cashews and mix well. Cover tightly and leave to marinate for at least 2 hours, stirring occasionally.

3 Heat the oil in a large, heavy-based skillet or wok. Remove the shrimp, scallions, and cashews from the marinade with a perforated spoon and add to the skillet or wok, reserving the marinade. Stir-fry over a high heat for 1–2 minutes.

4 Mix the reserved marinade with the cornstarch. Add to the skillet or wok and stir-fry for about 30 seconds, until the marinade forms a slightly thickened shiny glaze over the shrimp mixture.

5 Serve immediately, with rice and braised vegetables.

Step *1*

Step *2*

Step *4*

Shrimp Stir-Fry with Lemon Grass

*A very quick and tasty stir-fry using shrimp,
cucumber, and oyster mushrooms, flavored with lemon grass.*

SERVES 4

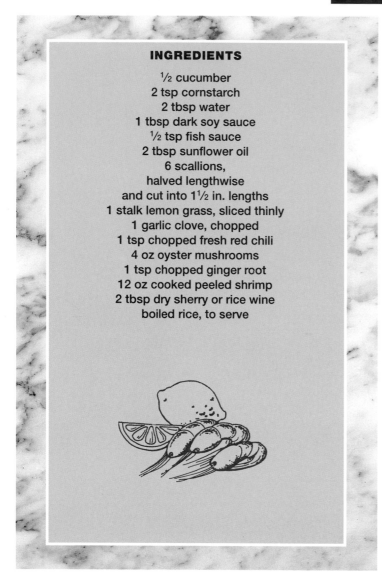

INGREDIENTS

½ cucumber
2 tsp cornstarch
2 tbsp water
1 tbsp dark soy sauce
½ tsp fish sauce
2 tbsp sunflower oil
6 scallions,
halved lengthwise
and cut into 1½ in. lengths
1 stalk lemon grass, sliced thinly
1 garlic clove, chopped
1 tsp chopped fresh red chili
4 oz oyster mushrooms
1 tsp chopped ginger root
12 oz cooked peeled shrimp
2 tbsp dry sherry or rice wine
boiled rice, to serve

1 Cut the cucumber into thin strips measuring about ¼ x 1¾ inches.

2 Mix together the cornstarch, water, soy sauce, and fish sauce until smooth and set aside.

3 Heat the oil in a wok or large skillet, add the scallions, cucumber, lemon grass, garlic, chili, mushrooms, and ginger, and stir-fry for 2 minutes.

4 Add the shrimp and stir-fry for a further minute.

5 Stir the cornstarch mixture and dry sherry or rice wine into the wok or skillet and heat through, stirring, until the sauce has thickened. Serve immediately with boiled rice.

Step *1*

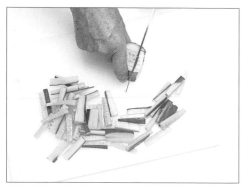

Step *3*

Step *5*

Sweet & Sour Shrimp with Chili

Use raw shrimp if possible.
Omit steps 1 and 2 if ready-cooked ones are used.

SERVES 4

INGREDIENTS

6–8 oz peeled raw tiger shrimp
pinch of salt
1 tsp egg white
1 tsp Cornstarch Paste (page 16)
1¼ cups vegetable oil

SAUCE

1 tbsp vegetable oil
½ small green bell pepper, cored,
deseeded, and sliced thinly
½ small carrot, sliced thinly
4 oz canned water chestnuts,
drained and sliced
½–1 tsp salt
1 tbsp light soy sauce
2 tbsp sugar
3 tbsp rice or sherry vinegar
1 tsp rice wine or dry sherry
1 tbsp tomato sauce
½–1 tsp chili sauce
3–4 tbsp Chinese Stock
(page 16) or water
2 tsp Cornstarch Paste (page 16)
a few drops of sesame oil

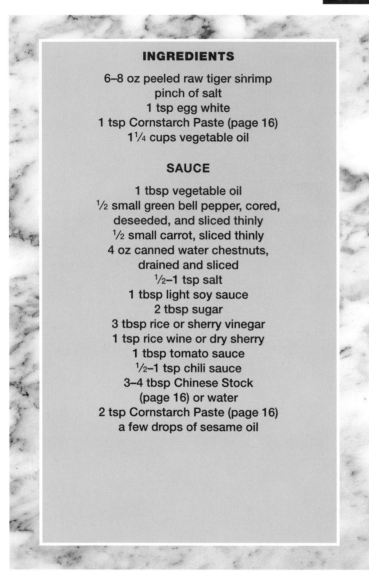

1 Mix the shrimp with the salt, egg white, and cornstarch paste.

2 Heat the oil in a preheated wok and stir-fry the shrimp for 30–40 seconds only. Remove and drain on paper towels.

3 Pour off the oil and wipe the wok clean with paper towels. To make the sauce, first heat the tablespoon of oil. Add the vegetables and stir-fry for about 1 minute, then add the seasonings with the stock or water, and bring to a boil.

4 Add the shrimp and stir until well blended. Thicken the sauce with the cornstarch paste and stir until smooth. Sprinkle with sesame oil and serve hot.

Step *2*

Step *3*

Step *4*

Sweet & Sour Shrimp

*Use raw shrimp if possible; ready-cooked ones can be added to the sauce
without the initial deep-frying (step 2).*

SERVES 4

INGREDIENTS

10–12 oz raw jumbo or tiger shrimp
in their shells
vegetable oil for deep-frying
fresh cilantro leaves, to garnish

SAUCE

1 tbsp vegetable oil
2 tsp finely chopped scallions
1 tsp finely chopped ginger root
1 tbsp light soy sauce
2 tbsp sugar
3 tbsp rice vinegar
1 tsp Chinese rice wine or dry sherry
½ cup Chinese Stock
(page 16) or water
1 tbsp Cornstarch Paste (page 16)
a few drops of sesame oil
cilantro leaves, to garnish

1 Remove the legs from the shrimp but leave the body shell in place.

2 Heat the oil in a preheated wok. Deep-fry the shrimp in hot oil for about 45–50 seconds, or until they become bright orange. Remove with a perforated spoon and drain on paper towels.

3 To make the sauce, heat the oil in a preheated wok and add the scallions and ginger, followed by the soy sauce, sugar, rice vinegar, wine, and stock or water. Bring to a boil.

4 Add the shrimp to the sauce, blend well, then thicken the sauce with the cornstarch paste. Stir until smooth and add the sesame oil.

5 Serve hot, garnished with cilantro leaves.

Step *2*

Step *3*

Step *4*

Baked Crab with Ginger

The crab is interchangeable with lobster. In Chinese restaurants, only live crabs and lobsters are used, but ready-cooked ones can be used at home.

SERVES 4

INGREDIENTS

1 large or 2 medium crabs,
weighing about 1½ lb in total
2 tbsp Chinese rice wine or dry sherry
1 egg, lightly beaten
1 tbsp cornstarch
3–4 tbsp vegetable oil
1 tbsp finely chopped ginger root
3–4 scallions, cut into sections
2 tbsp light soy sauce
1 tsp sugar
about ⅓ cup Chinese Stock (page 16)
or water
½ tsp sesame oil
cilantro leaves, to garnish

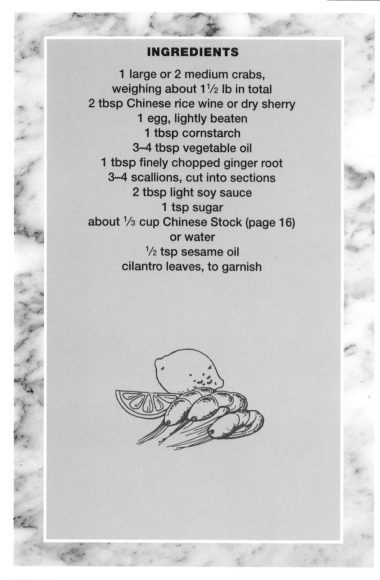

1 Cut the crab in half from the underbelly. Break off the claws and crack them with the back of the cleaver or a large kitchen knife.

2 Discard the legs and crack the shell, breaking it into several pieces. Discard the feathery gills and the stomach sac. Place in a bowl with the wine, egg, and cornstarch and leave to marinate for 10–15 minutes.

3 Heat the oil in a preheated wok and stir-fry the crab with the ginger and scallions for 2–3 minutes.

4 Add the soy sauce, sugar, and stock or water, blend well, and bring to a boil. Cover and cook for 3–4 minutes, then remove the cover. Sprinkle with sesame oil and garnish with cilantro before serving.

Step *1*

Step *2*

Step *4*

Spiced Scallops

Scallops are available both fresh and frozen.
Make sure they are completely defrosted before cooking.

SERVES 4

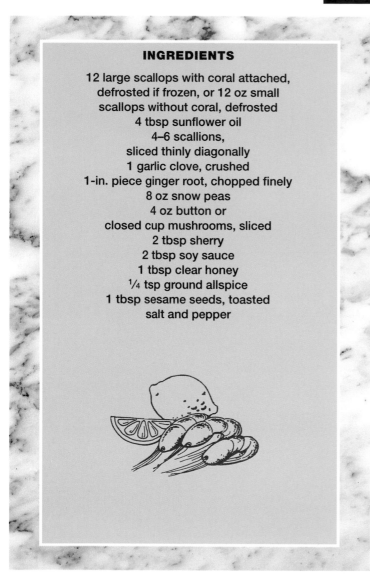

INGREDIENTS

12 large scallops with coral attached,
defrosted if frozen, or 12 oz small
scallops without coral, defrosted
4 tbsp sunflower oil
4–6 scallions,
sliced thinly diagonally
1 garlic clove, crushed
1-in. piece ginger root, chopped finely
8 oz snow peas
4 oz button or
closed cup mushrooms, sliced
2 tbsp sherry
2 tbsp soy sauce
1 tbsp clear honey
¼ tsp ground allspice
1 tbsp sesame seeds, toasted
salt and pepper

1 Wash and dry the scallops, discarding any black pieces. Detach the corals, if using. Slice each scallop into 3–4 pieces and halve the corals if they are large.

2 Heat 2 tablespoons of oil in the wok, swirling it around until really hot. Add the scallions, garlic, and ginger, and stir-fry for a minute or so. Add the snow peas and continue to stir-fry for 2–3 minutes. Remove to a bowl.

3 Add the remaining oil to the wok. When really hot add the scallops and corals, and stir-fry for a couple of minutes. Add the mushrooms and continue to cook for a further minute or so.

4 Add the sherry, soy sauce, honey, and allspice to the wok, with salt and pepper to taste. Mix thoroughly, then return the vegetable mixture to the wok.

5 Season well and toss together over a high heat for a minute or so until piping hot. Serve immediately, sprinkled with sesame seeds.

Step *1*

Step *2*

Step *3*

Fried Squid Flowers

The addition of green bell pepper and black bean sauce to the squid makes a colorful and delicious dish from the Cantonese school.

SERVES 4

INGREDIENTS

12–14 oz prepared and cleaned squid
1 green bell pepper,
cored and deseeded
3–4 tbsp vegetable oil
1 garlic clove, chopped finely
¼ tsp finely chopped ginger root
2 tsp finely chopped scallions
½ tsp salt
2 tbsp crushed black bean sauce
1 tsp Chinese rice wine or dry sherry
a few drops of sesame oil

1 Open up the squid and score the inside of the flesh in a criss-cross pattern.

2 Cut the squid into pieces about 1 x 1½ inches. Blanch in a bowl of boiling water for a few seconds. Drain and dry well on paper towels.

3 Cut the bell pepper into small triangular pieces. Heat the oil in a preheated wok and stir-fry the bell pepper for about 1 minute. Add the garlic, ginger, scallion, salt, and squid. Continue stirring for another minute.

4 Finally add the black bean sauce and wine, and blend well. Serve hot, sprinkled with sesame oil.

Step *1*

Step *3*

Step *4*

Fish with Black Bean Sauce

*Any firm fish and steaks, such as salmon
or turbot, can be cooked by the same method.*

SERVES 4–6

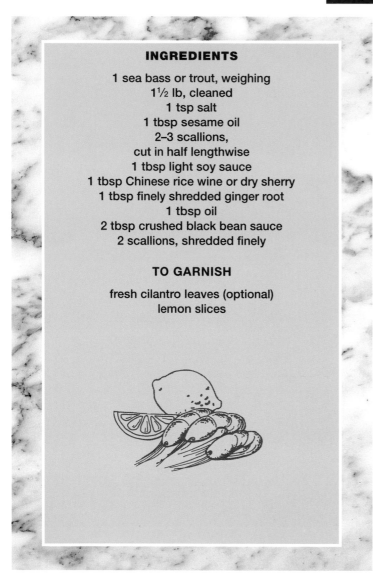

INGREDIENTS

1 sea bass or trout, weighing
1½ lb, cleaned
1 tsp salt
1 tbsp sesame oil
2–3 scallions,
cut in half lengthwise
1 tbsp light soy sauce
1 tbsp Chinese rice wine or dry sherry
1 tbsp finely shredded ginger root
1 tbsp oil
2 tbsp crushed black bean sauce
2 scallions, shredded finely

TO GARNISH

fresh cilantro leaves (optional)
lemon slices

1 Score both sides of the fish with diagonal cuts at 1 in. intervals. Rub both the inside and outside of the fish with the salt and sesame oil.

2 Place the fish on top of the scallions on a heatproof platter. Blend the soy sauce and wine with the ginger shreds and pour evenly all over the fish.

3 Place the fish on the platter in a very hot steamer (or inside a wok on a rack). Cover and steam vigorously for 12–15 minutes.

4 Heat the oil in a wok or saucepan until hot, then blend in the black bean sauce. Remove the fish from the steamer and place on a serving dish. Pour the hot black bean sauce over the whole length of the fish, and place the shredded scallions on top. Serve garnished with cilantro leaves, if using, and lemon slices.

Step *2*

Step *3*

Step *4*

Braised Fish Fillets

Any white fish, such as lemon sole or plaice, is ideal for this dish.

SERVES 4

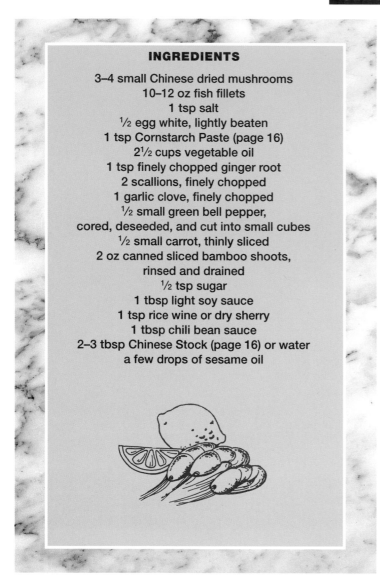

INGREDIENTS

3–4 small Chinese dried mushrooms
10–12 oz fish fillets
1 tsp salt
½ egg white, lightly beaten
1 tsp Cornstarch Paste (page 16)
2½ cups vegetable oil
1 tsp finely chopped ginger root
2 scallions, finely chopped
1 garlic clove, finely chopped
½ small green bell pepper,
cored, deseeded, and cut into small cubes
½ small carrot, thinly sliced
2 oz canned sliced bamboo shoots,
rinsed and drained
½ tsp sugar
1 tbsp light soy sauce
1 tsp rice wine or dry sherry
1 tbsp chili bean sauce
2–3 tbsp Chinese Stock (page 16) or water
a few drops of sesame oil

1 Soak the dried mushrooms in warm water for 30 minutes, then drain on paper towels, reserving the soaking water for stock or soup. Squeeze the mushrooms to extract all the moisture, cut off and discard any hard stems, and slice thinly.

2 Cut the fish into bite-size pieces, then place in a shallow dish, and mix with a pinch of salt, the egg white, and cornstarch paste, turning the fish to coat well.

3 Heat the oil and deep-fry the fish pieces for about 1 minute. Remove with a perforated spoon and drain on paper towels.

4 Pour off the oil, leaving about 1 tablespoon in the wok. Add the ginger, scallions, and garlic to flavor the oil for a few seconds, then add the vegetables, and stir-fry for about 1 minute.

5 Add the sugar, soy sauce, wine, chili bean sauce, stock or water, and remaining salt, and bring to a boil. Add the fish pieces, stir to coat well with the sauce, and braise for another minute. Sprinkle with sesame oil and serve immediately.

Step *3*

Step *4*

Step *5*

Fish in Szechuan Hot Sauce

*This is a classic Szechuan recipe. When served in a restaurant, the fish
head and tail are removed before cooking.*

SERVES 4

INGREDIENTS

1 carp, bream, sea bass, trout,
grouper, or grey mullet, about 1½ lb, gutted
1 tbsp light soy sauce
1 tbsp Chinese rice wine or dry sherry
vegetable oil for deep-frying
flat-leaf parsley or cilantro sprigs,
to garnish

SAUCE

2 garlic cloves, chopped finely
2–3 scallions, chopped finely
1 tsp finely chopped ginger root
2 tbsp chili bean sauce
1 tbsp tomato paste
2 tsp sugar
1 tbsp rice vinegar
½ cup Chinese Stock
(see page 16) or water
1 tbsp Cornstarch Paste (page 16)
½ tsp sesame oil

1 Wash the fish and dry well on paper towels. Score both sides of the fish to the bone with a sharp knife, making diagonal cuts at intervals of about 1 in. Rub the fish with the soy sauce and wine on both sides, then leave on a plate in the refrigerator to marinate for 10–15 minutes.

2 Heat the oil in a preheated wok until smoking. Deep-fry the fish in the hot oil for about 3–4 minutes on both sides, or until golden brown.

3 Pour off the oil, leaving about 1 tablespoon in the wok. Push the fish to one side of the wok and add the garlic, white parts of the scallions, ginger, chili bean sauce, tomato paste, sugar, vinegar, and stock. Bring to a boil and braise the fish in the sauce for 4–5 minutes, turning it over once.

4 Add the green parts of the scallions and stir in the cornstarch paste to thicken the sauce. Sprinkle with sesame oil and serve at once, garnished with parsley or cilantro.

Step *1*

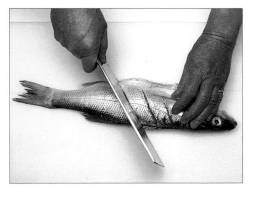

Step *2*

Step *3*

POULTRY DISHES

Second to pork, poultry is one of the most popular foods throughout China. It also plays an important symbolic role. The cock symbolizes the male, positiveness, and aggression; the duck represents happiness and fidelity; and the pigeon filial concern and longevity. Duck would be the most popular choice at a banquet, but chicken, goose, and pheasant are also eaten in quantity.

Being uniformly tender, poultry is ideal for Chinese cooking methods, since these rely on the rapid cooking of ingredients and small, uniformly-sized pieces of meat. Poultry can easily be cut into wafer-thin slices, thin matchstick strips, or cubes, and can be quickly cooked without any loss of moisture or tenderness.

Poultry is always purchased live in China, killed at home, and plucked by hand. Since this is not normally possible in the West, always look for birds with plump, springy flesh and smooth, dry skin. The breastbone should be flexible and springy. It is cheaper to buy a whole chicken which can then be easily cut into smaller serving pieces ready for stir-frying, braising, or steaming.

Aromatic & Crispy Duck

The pancakes traditionally served with this dish take ages to make. Buy ready-made ones from oriental stores, or use crisp lettuce instead.

SERVES 4

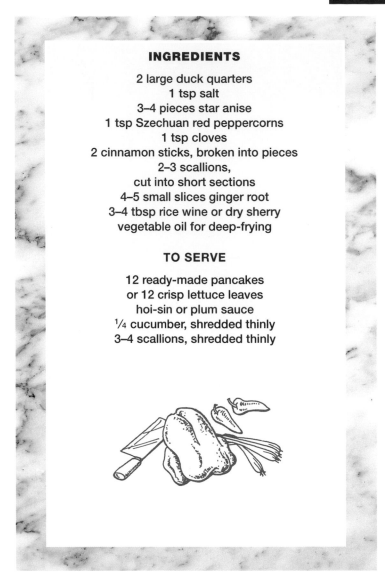

INGREDIENTS

2 large duck quarters
1 tsp salt
3–4 pieces star anise
1 tsp Szechuan red peppercorns
1 tsp cloves
2 cinnamon sticks, broken into pieces
2–3 scallions,
cut into short sections
4–5 small slices ginger root
3–4 tbsp rice wine or dry sherry
vegetable oil for deep-frying

TO SERVE

12 ready-made pancakes
or 12 crisp lettuce leaves
hoi-sin or plum sauce
¼ cucumber, shredded thinly
3–4 scallions, shredded thinly

1 Rub the duck pieces with the salt and arrange the star anise, peppercorns, cloves, and cinnamon on top. Sprinkle with the scallions, ginger, and wine and leave to marinate for at least 3–4 hours.

2 Arrange the duck pieces (with the marinade spices) on a plate that will fit inside a bamboo steamer. Pour some hot water into a wok, place the bamboo steamer in the wok, sitting on a trivet. Put in the duck and cover with the bamboo lid. Steam the duck pieces (with the marinade) over high heat for at least 2–3 hours, until tender and cooked through. Top up the hot water from time to time as required.

3 Remove the duck and leave to cool for at least 4–5 hours – this is very important, for unless the duck is cold and dry, it will not be crisp.

4 Pour off the water and wipe the wok dry. Pour in the oil and heat until smoking. Deep-fry the duck pieces, skin-side down, for 4–5 minutes or until crisp and brown. Remove and drain on paper towels.

5 To serve, scrape the meat off the bone, place about 1 teaspoon of hoi-sin or plum sauce on the center of a pancake (or lettuce leaf), add a few pieces of cucumber and scallion, with a portion of the duck meat. Wrap up to form a small package and eat with your fingers. Provide plenty of paper napkins for your guests.

Step *1*

Step *2*

Step *4*

Duck with Pineapple

For best results, use ready-cooked duck meat,
widely available from Chinese restaurants and stores.

SERVES 4

INGREDIENTS

4–6 oz cooked duck meat
3 tbsp vegetable oil
1 small onion, shredded thinly
2–3 slices ginger root, shredded thinly
1 scallion, shredded thinly
1 small carrot, shredded thinly
4 oz canned pineapple, cut into small slices
½ tsp salt
1 tbsp red rice vinegar
2 tbsp syrup from the pineapple
1 tbsp Cornstarch Paste (page 16)
black bean sauce, to serve (optional)

1 Cut the cooked duck meat into thin strips using a Chinese cleaver or very sharp knife.

2 Heat the oil in a preheated wok, add the onion, and stir-fry until the shreds are opaque. Add the ginger, scallion, and carrot. Stir-fry for 1 minute.

3 Add the duck shreds and pineapple to the wok, together with the salt, rice vinegar, and the pineapple syrup. Stir until the mixture is blended well.

4 Add the cornstarch paste and stir for 1–2 minutes until the sauce has thickened. Serve hot.

Step *1*

Step *2*

Step *4*

Kung Po Chicken with Cashew Nuts

Peanuts, walnuts, or almonds can be used instead
of the cashew nuts, if preferred.

SERVES 4

INGREDIENTS

8–10 oz boned and skinned
chicken meat
¼ tsp salt
⅓ egg white
1 tsp Cornstarch Paste (page 16)
1 green bell pepper,
cored and deseeded
4 tbsp vegetable oil
1 scallion, cut into short sections
a few small slices of ginger root
4–5 small dried red chilies, soaked,
deseeded, and shredded
2 tbsp crushed yellow bean sauce
1 tsp rice wine or dry sherry
4 oz roasted cashew nuts
a few drops of sesame oil
boiled rice, to serve

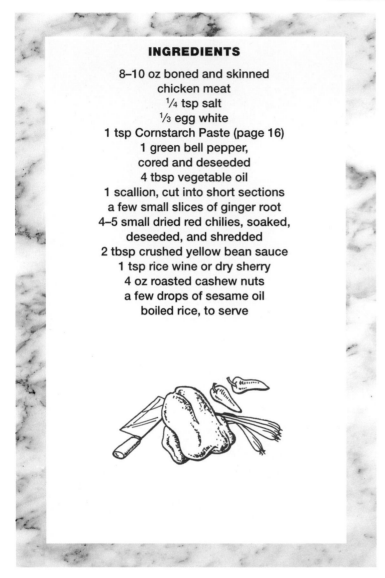

1 Cut the chicken into small cubes about the size of sugar lumps. Place in a small bowl and mix with a pinch of salt, the egg white, and the cornstarch paste, in that order.

2 Cut the green bell pepper into cubes or triangles about the same size as the chicken pieces.

3 Heat the oil in a preheated wok, add the chicken cubes, and stir-fry for about 1 minute, or until the color changes. Remove with a perforated spoon and keep warm.

4 Add the scallion, ginger, chilies, and green bell pepper. Stir-fry for about 1 minute, then add the chicken with the yellow bean sauce and wine. Blend well and stir-fry for another minute. Finally stir in the cashew nuts and sesame oil. Serve hot.

Step *1*

Step *2*

Step *4*

Chicken with Bean-Sprouts

This is the basic Chicken Chop Suey to be found in almost every Chinese restaurant all over the world.

SERVES 4

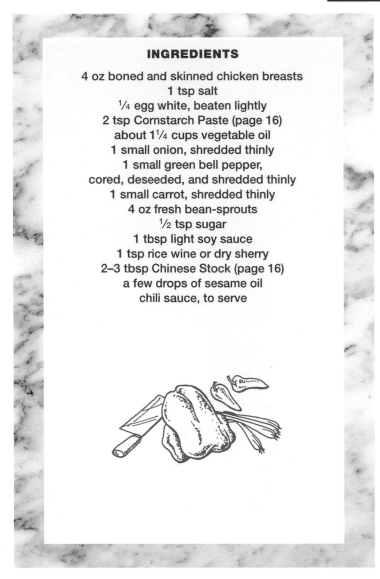

INGREDIENTS

4 oz boned and skinned chicken breasts
1 tsp salt
¼ egg white, beaten lightly
2 tsp Cornstarch Paste (page 16)
about 1¼ cups vegetable oil
1 small onion, shredded thinly
1 small green bell pepper,
cored, deseeded, and shredded thinly
1 small carrot, shredded thinly
4 oz fresh bean-sprouts
½ tsp sugar
1 tbsp light soy sauce
1 tsp rice wine or dry sherry
2–3 tbsp Chinese Stock (page 16)
a few drops of sesame oil
chili sauce, to serve

1 Thinly shred the chicken and mix with a pinch of the salt, the egg white, and cornstarch paste in that order.

2 Heat the oil in a preheated wok and stir-fry the chicken for about 1 minute until no longer pink, stirring to separate the shreds. Remove with a perforated spoon and drain on paper towels.

3 Pour off the oil, leaving about 2 tablespoons in the wok. Add all the vegetables except the bean-sprouts, and stir-fry for about 2 minutes. Then add the bean-sprouts and stir for a few seconds.

4 Add the chicken with the remaining salt, sugar, soy sauce, and wine. Blend well and add the stock or water. Sprinkle with the sesame oil and serve at once.

Step *2*

Step *3*

Step *4*

Lemon Chicken

*Lemon sauce is a Cantonese speciality, easily available from
Oriental stores, or you can make your own.*

SERVES 4

INGREDIENTS

12 oz boned and skinned
chicken breasts
1 tbsp rice wine or dry sherry
1 egg, beaten
4 tbsp all-purpose flour blended with 2 tbsp water
vegetable oil for deep-frying
salt and pepper
slices of fresh lemon, to garnish

LEMON SAUCE

1 tbsp vegetable oil
1 cup Chinese Stock (page 16)
1 tbsp superfine sugar
1 tbsp lemon juice
1 tbsp cornstarch
1 tsp salt
1 tsp lemon rind

1 To make the lemon sauce, heat the oil in a wok until hot, reduce the heat, and add all the other ingredients. Blend well, then bring to a boil, and stir until smooth.

2 Cut the chicken into thin slices and place in a shallow dish with the wine, and salt and pepper. Leave to marinate for 25–30 minutes.

3 Make a batter with the egg and the flour paste. Place the chicken slices in the batter and turn to coat well.

4 Heat the oil in a wok or deep-fryer. Deep-fry the chicken slices until golden brown, remove with a perforated spoon, and drain on paper towels. Cut the chicken slices into bite-size pieces.

5 Heat about 1 tablespoon of oil in a wok or pan. Stir in the lemon sauce until well blended and pour evenly over the chicken. Garnish with lemon slices.

Step *1*

Step *3*

Step *4*

Peanut Sesame Chicken

*A quick-to-make chicken and vegetable dish. Sesame and peanuts give it
crunch and the fruit juice glaze gives a lovely shiny coating to the sauce.*

SERVES 4

INGREDIENTS

2 tbsp vegetable oil
2 tbsp sesame oil
1 lb boned and skinned chicken
breasts, sliced into strips
8 oz broccoli, divided into small flowerets
8 oz baby or dwarf corncobs,
halved if large
1 small red bell pepper,
cored, deseeded, and sliced
2 tbsp soy sauce
1 cup orange juice
2 tsp cornstarch
2 tbsp toasted sesame seeds
⅓ cup roasted,
shelled, unsalted peanuts
rice or noodles, to serve

1 Heat the oils in a large, heavy-based skillet or wok, add the chicken strips, and stir-fry until browned, about 4–5 minutes.

2 Add the broccoli, corn, and red bell pepper and stir-fry for a further 1–2 minutes.

3 Meanwhile, mix the soy sauce with the orange juice and cornstarch. Stir into the chicken and vegetable mixture, stirring constantly until the sauce has slightly thickened and a glaze develops.

4 Stir in the sesame seeds and peanuts, mixing well. Heat for a further 3–4 minutes. Serve at once, with rice or noodles.

Step *1*

Step *2*

Step *3*

Chicken with Bell Pepper

The bell pepper can be replaced with celery – the method is exactly the same.

SERVES 4

INGREDIENTS

10 oz boned and skinned chicken breasts
1 tsp salt
½ egg white
2 tsp Cornstarch Paste (page 16)
1 green bell pepper,
cored and deseeded
1¼ cups vegetable oil
1 scallion, shredded finely
a few strips of ginger root, shredded finely
1–2 red chilies, deseeded and shredded finely
½ tsp sugar
1 tbsp rice wine or dry sherry
a few drops of sesame oil

1 Cut the chicken breasts into strips, then mix in a bowl with a pinch of the salt, the egg white, and cornstarch, in that order.

2 Cut the bell pepper into thin shreds the same size and length as the chicken strips.

3 Heat the oil in a preheated wok, and deep-fry the chicken strips in batches for about 1 minute, or until no longer pink. Remove the chicken strips with a perforated spoon and keep warm.

4 Pour off the excess oil from the wok, leaving about 1 tablespoon. Add the scallion, ginger, chilies, and bell pepper. Stir-fry for about 1 minute, then return the chicken to the wok. Add the remaining salt, the sugar, and wine. Stir-fry for another minute, sprinkle with sesame oil, and serve.

Step 2

Step 3

Step 4

Chicken Foo-Yung

A foo-yung dish should use egg whites only to create a very delicate texture. But most people associate foo-yung with an omelet.

SERVES 4

INGREDIENTS

6 oz boned and skinned chicken breasts
1 tsp rice wine or dry sherry
1 tbsp cornstarch
3 eggs, beaten
½ tsp finely chopped scallions
3 tbsp vegetable oil
4 oz green peas
1 tsp light soy sauce
few drops of sesame oil
salt and pepper

1 Cut the chicken across the grain into very small, paper-thin slices, using the cleaver. Place the chicken slices in a shallow dish, add ½ teaspoon salt, pepper, the wine, and cornstarch, and turn in the mixture until they are well coated.

2 Beat the eggs in a small bowl with a pinch of salt and the scallions.

3 Heat the oil in a preheated wok, add the chicken slices, and stir-fry for about 1 minute, making sure that the slices are kept separated. Pour the beaten eggs over the chicken, and lightly scramble until set. Do not stir too vigorously, or the mixture will break up in the oil. Stir the oil from the bottom of the wok so that the foo-yung rises to the surface.

4 Add the peas, soy sauce, and salt to taste and blend well. Sprinkle with sesame oil and serve.

Step *2*

Step *3*

Step *4*

Bang-Bang Chicken

*The cooked chicken meat is tenderized by beating with a rolling pin,
hence the name for this very popular Szechuan dish.*

SERVES 4

INGREDIENTS

4 cups water
2 chicken quarters (breast half and leg)
1 cucumber, cut into matchstick shreds

SAUCE

2 tbsp light soy sauce
1 tsp sugar
1 tbsp finely chopped scallions
1 tsp red chili oil
¼ tsp pepper
1 tsp white sesame seeds
2 tbsp peanut butter,
creamed with a little sesame oil

1 Bring the water to a rolling boil in a wok or a large pan. Add the chicken pieces, reduce the heat, cover, and cook for 30–35 minutes.

2 Remove the chicken from the pan and immerse it in a bowl of cold water for at least 1 hour to cool it, ready for shredding.

3 Remove the chicken pieces and drain well. Pat dry with paper towels, then take the meat off the bone.

4 On a flat surface, pound the chicken with a rolling pin, then tear the meat into shreds with 2 forks. Mix with the shredded cucumber and arrange in a shallow serving dish.

5 To serve, mix together all the sauce ingredients and pour over the chicken.

Step *1*

Step *2*

Step *4*

Szechuan Chili Chicken

*In China, the chicken pieces are chopped through the bone for this dish,
but if you do not possess a cleaver, use filleted chicken meat.*

SERVES 4

INGREDIENTS

1 lb chicken thighs
¼ tsp pepper
1 tbsp sugar
2 tsp light soy sauce
1 tsp dark soy sauce
1 tbsp rice wine or dry sherry
2 tsp cornstarch
2–3 tbsp vegetable oil
1–2 garlic cloves, crushed
2 scallions,
cut into short sections,
with the green and white parts separated
4–6 small dried red chilies, soaked and deseeded
2 tbsp yellow bean sauce
⅔ cup Chinese Stock (page 16)
or water

1 Cut or chop the chicken thighs into bite-size pieces. Marinate with the pepper, sugar, soy sauce, wine, and cornstarch for 25–30 minutes.

2 Heat the oil in a preheated wok, add the chicken pieces, and stir-fry until lightly brown for about 1–2 minutes. Remove the chicken pieces with a perforated spoon, transfer to a warm dish, and reserve.

3 Add the garlic, the white parts of the scallions, the chilies, and yellow bean sauce. Stir-fry for about 30 seconds, blending well.

4 Return the chicken pieces to the wok and stir-fry for about 1–2 minutes. Add the stock or water, bring to a boil, and cover. Braise over medium heat for 5–6 minutes, stirring once or twice. Garnish with the green parts of the scallions and serve immediately.

Step *2*

Step *3*

Step *4*

Chicken with Mushrooms

Chinese dried mushrooms (shiitake) should be used for this dish – otherwise use fresh shiitake rather than fresh white mushrooms.

SERVES 4

INGREDIENTS

10–12 oz boned and skinned
chicken breasts
½ tsp sugar
1 tbsp light soy sauce
1 tsp rice wine or dry sherry
2 tsp cornstarch
4–6 Chinese dried mushrooms,
soaked in warm water for 30 minutes
1 tbsp finely shredded ginger root
salt and pepper
a few drops of sesame oil
cilantro leaves, to garnish

1 Cut the chicken into bite-size pieces and place in a bowl. Add the sugar, soy sauce, wine, and cornstarch. Leave to marinate for 25–30 minutes.

2 Drain the mushrooms and dry on paper towels. Slice the mushrooms into thin shreds, discarding any hard pieces of stem.

3 Place the chicken pieces on a heatproof dish that will fit inside a bamboo steamer. Arrange the mushroom and ginger shreds on top of the chicken and sprinkle with salt, pepper, and sesame oil.

4 Place the dish on the rack inside a hot steamer or on a rack in a wok filled with hot water and steam over high heat for 20 minutes. Serve hot, garnished with cilantro leaves.

Step *1*

Step *2*

Step *4*

Chicken with Celery & Cashews Nuts

Yellow bean sauce, widely available in bottles, gives this quick and easy dish a really authentic taste. Pecan nuts can be used in place of cashews.

SERVES 4

INGREDIENTS

1¼ lb boned and skinned chicken breasts
2 tbsp sunflower or vegetable oil
1 cup (unsalted) cashew nuts
4–6 scallions,
sliced thinly diagonally
5–6 celery stalks, sliced thinly diagonally
6 oz jar yellow bean sauce
salt and pepper
boiled rice, to serve
celery leaves, to garnish (optional)

1 Cut the chicken into thin slices across the grain using a Chinese cleaver or very sharp knife.

2 Heat the oil in the wok, swirling it around until really hot. Add the cashew nuts and stir-fry until they begin to brown, then add the chicken, and stir-fry until well sealed and almost cooked through.

3 Add the scallions and celery and continue to stir-fry for 2–3 minutes, stirring the food around the wok.

4 Add the yellow bean sauce, season lightly, and toss until the chicken and vegetables are thoroughly coated with the sauce and piping hot.

5 Serve at once with plain boiled rice, garnished with celery leaves, if liked.

Step *2*

Step *3*

Step *4*

MEAT DISHES

In Chinese cooking, pork is the most popular of all meats. A whole roasted pig, with its skin cracking and burnished, is an essential feature at a Chinese wedding feast or New Year celebration. Lamb is popular in northern China where religious laws forbid the eating of pork. Although it is used in some dishes, beef is less popular with the Chinese than pork. This is partly because of economic and religious issues, but also because beef is less versatile in cooking. Only certain cuts, such as tenderloin and sirloin, are tender enough for stir-frying. However, these prime cuts tend to dry out and toughen during slow moist cooking. For braising and stewing the most satisfactory cuts are the less tender ones, such as brisket.

Because pork is tender regardless of cut, it is ideally suited to all Chinese cooking methods. Stir-frying is a simple and easy way of preparing meat, as well as being economical, delicious, and healthy. Braising and steaming are also popular methods of cooking meat, ensuring a tender result, and so too is double-cooking. This is a technique in which the meat is first tenderized by long, slow simmering in water, followed by a quick crisping or stir-frying in a sauce – Twice-Cooked Pork (page 158) is a delicious example of this technique.

Beef & Bok Choy

A colorful selection of vegetables stir-fried with tender strips of steak.

SERVES 4

INGREDIENTS

1 large head of bok choy,
8–9 oz, torn into large pieces
2 tbsp vegetable oil
2 garlic cloves, crushed
1 lb sirloin or fillet steak,
cut into thin strips
5 oz snow peas, trimmed
5 oz baby or dwarf corncobs
6 scallions, chopped
2 red bell peppers, cored,
deseeded, and thinly sliced
2 tbsp oyster sauce
1 tbsp fish sauce
1 tbsp sugar
rice or noodles, to serve

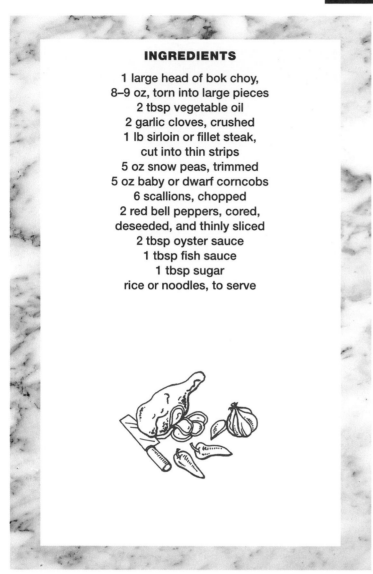

1 Steam the bok choy leaves over boiling water until just tender. Keep warm.

2 Heat the oil in a large, heavy-based skillet or wok, add the garlic and steak strips, and stir-fry until just browned, about 1–2 minutes.

3 Add the snow peas, baby corncobs, scallions, bell pepper, oyster sauce, fish sauce, and sugar, mixing well. Stir-fry for a further 2–3 minutes until the vegetables are just tender, but still crisp.

4 Arrange the bok choy leaves in the base of a warm serving dish and spoon the beef and vegetable mixture into the center.

5 Serve the stir-fry immediately, with rice or noodles.

Step *1*

Step *2*

Step *3*

Beef & Chili Black Bean Sauce

It is not necessary to use the expensive cuts of beef steak for this recipe: the meat will be tender as it is cut into small thin slices and marinated.

SERVES 4

INGREDIENTS

8–10 oz beef steak
1 small onion
1 small green bell pepper,
cored and deseeded
about 1¼ cups vegetable oil
1 scallion,
cut into short sections
a few small slices of ginger root
1–2 small green or red chilies,
deseeded and sliced
2 tbsp crushed black bean sauce

MARINADE

½ tsp bicarbonate of soda
or baking powder
½ tsp sugar
1 tbsp light soy sauce
2 tsp rice wine or dry sherry
2 tsp Cornstarch Paste (page 16)
2 tsp sesame oil

1 Cut the beef into small thin strips. Mix together the marinade ingredients in a shallow dish, add the beef strips, turn to coat, and leave to marinate for at least 2–3 hours – the longer the better.

2 Cut the onion and green bell pepper into small equal-size squares.

3 Heat the oil in a preheated wok. Add the beef strips and stir-fry for about 1 minute, or until the color changes. Remove with a perforated spoon and drain on paper towels. Keep warm.

4 Pour off the excess oil, leaving about 1 tablespoon in the wok. Add the scallion, ginger, chilies, onion, and green bell pepper and stir-fry for about 1 minute. Add the black bean sauce, stir until smooth, then return the beef strips to the wok. Blend well and stir-fry for another minute. Serve hot.

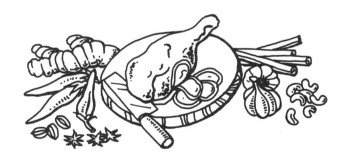

Step *2*

Step *3*

Step *4*

Peppered Beef Cashew

A simple but stunning dish of tender strips of beef mixed with crunchy cashew nuts, coated in a hot sauce. Serve with rice sticks.

SERVES 4

INGREDIENTS

1 tbsp groundnut or sunflower oil
1 tbsp sesame oil
1 onion, sliced
1 garlic clove, crushed
1 tbsp grated ginger root
1 lb tenderloin or sirloin steak,
cut into thin strips
2 tsp palm sugar or demerara sugar
2 tbsp light soy sauce
1 small yellow bell pepper,
cored, deseeded, and sliced
1 red bell pepper,
cored, deseeded, and sliced
4 scallions, chopped
2 celery stalks, chopped
4 large open-cap mushrooms, sliced
4 tbsp roasted cashew nuts
3 tbsp stock or white wine
rice noodles, to serve

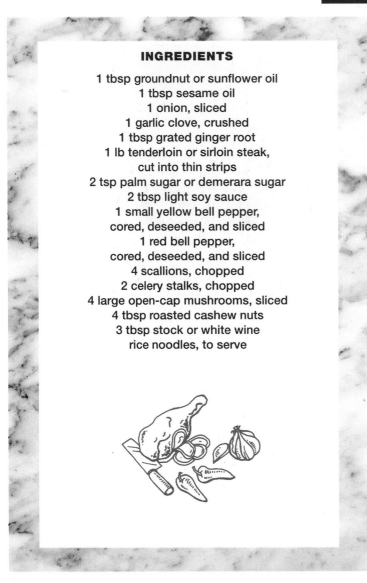

1 Heat the oils in a wok or large, heavy-based skillet. Add the onion, garlic, and ginger, and stir-fry for about 2 minutes until softened and lightly colored.

2 Add the steak strips and stir-fry for a further 2–3 minutes, until the meat has browned.

3 Add the sugar and soy sauce, mixing well.

4 Add the bell peppers, scallions, celery, mushrooms, and cashews, mixing well.

5 Add the stock or wine and stir-fry for 2–3 minutes until the beef is cooked through and the vegetables are tender-crisp. Serve immediately with rice sticks.

Step *1*

Step *2*

Step *5*

Red Spiced Beef

A spicy stir-fry flavored with paprika, chili, and tomato,
with a crisp bite to it from the celery strips.

SERVES 4

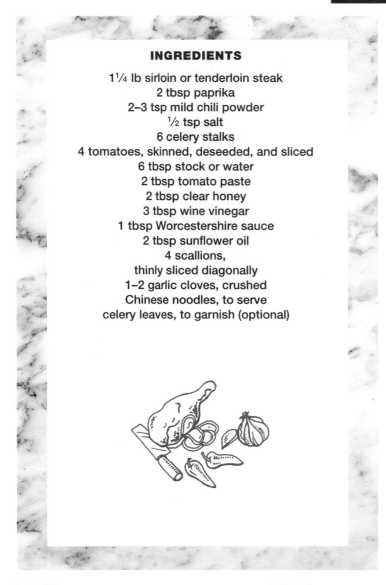

INGREDIENTS

1¼ lb sirloin or tenderloin steak
2 tbsp paprika
2–3 tsp mild chili powder
½ tsp salt
6 celery stalks
4 tomatoes, skinned, deseeded, and sliced
6 tbsp stock or water
2 tbsp tomato paste
2 tbsp clear honey
3 tbsp wine vinegar
1 tbsp Worcestershire sauce
2 tbsp sunflower oil
4 scallions,
thinly sliced diagonally
1–2 garlic cloves, crushed
Chinese noodles, to serve
celery leaves, to garnish (optional)

1 Cut the steak across the grain into narrow strips ½ in. thick and place in a bowl. Combine the paprika, chili powder, and salt. Add to the beef and mix thoroughly until the meat strips are evenly coated with the spices. Cover and leave to marinate in a cool place for at least 30 minutes.

2 Cut the celery into 2 in. lengths, then slice into strips about ¼ in. thick. Combine the stock, tomato paste, honey, vinegar, and Worcestershire sauce.

3 Heat the oil in the wok, swirling it around until really hot. Add the scallions, celery, and garlic, and stir-fry for about 1 minute until the vegetables are beginning to soften. Then add the steak strips and stir-fry over a high heat for 3–4 minutes until the meat is well sealed.

4 Add the sauce to the wok and continue to stir-fry briskly until thoroughly coated and sizzling.

5 Serve with noodles and garnish with celery leaves, if liked.

Step *1*

Step *3*

Step *4*

Oyster Sauce Beef

As in Stir-Fried Pork with Vegetables (page 168), the vegetables can be varied as you wish.

SERVES 4

INGREDIENTS

10 oz beef steak
1 tsp sugar
1 tbsp light soy sauce
1 tsp rice wine or dry sherry
1 tsp Cornstarch Paste (page 16)
½ small carrot
2 oz snow peas
2 oz canned bamboo shoots
2 oz canned straw mushrooms
about 1¼ cups vegetable oil
1 scallion, cut into short sections
2–3 small slices ginger root
½ tsp salt
2 tbsp oyster sauce
2–3 tbsp Chinese Stock (page 16) or water

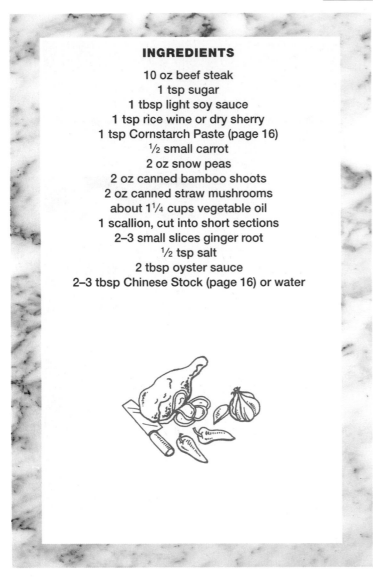

1 Cut the beef into small, thin slices. Place in a shallow dish with the sugar, soy sauce, wine, and cornstarch paste and leave to marinate for 25–30 minutes.

2 Slice the carrots, snow peas, bamboo shoots, and straw mushrooms so that as far as possible the vegetable pieces are of uniform size and thickness.

3 Heat the oil in a preheated wok and add the beef slices. Stir-fry for about 1 minute, then remove with a perforated spoon and keep warm.

4 Pour off the oil, leaving about 1 tablespoon in the wok. Add the sliced vegetables with the scallion and ginger, and stir-fry for about 2 minutes. Add the salt, beef, oyster sauce, and stock or water. Blend well until heated through, and serve.

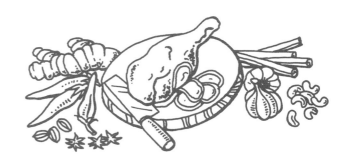

Step *2*

Step *3*

Step *4*

Crispy Shredded Beef

A very popular Szechuan dish served in most
Chinese restaurants all over the world.

SERVES 4

INGREDIENTS

10–12 oz beef steak
(such as round or sirloin)
2 eggs
¼ tsp salt
4–5 tbsp all-purpose flour
vegetable oil for deep-frying
2 medium carrots, shredded finely
2 scallions, shredded finely
1 garlic clove, chopped finely
2–3 small fresh green or red chilies,
deseeded and shredded finely
4 tbsp sugar
3 tbsp rice vinegar
1 tbsp light soy sauce
2–3 tbsp Chinese Stock (page 16) or water
1 tsp Cornstarch Paste (page 16)

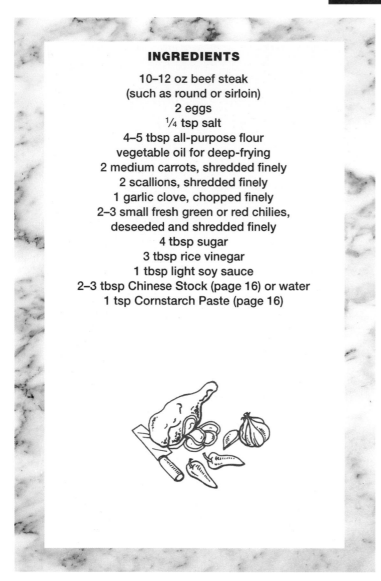

1 Cut the steak across the grain into thin strips. Beat the eggs in a bowl with the salt and flour, adding a little water if necessary. Add the beef strips and mix well until coated with the batter.

2 Heat the oil in a preheated wok until smoking. Add the beef strips and deep-fry for 4–5 minutes, stirring to separate the shreds. Remove with a perforated spoon and drain on paper towels.

3 Add the carrots to the wok and deep-fry for about 1–1½ minutes, then remove with a slotted spoon, and drain on paper towels.

4 Pour off the excess oil, leaving about 1 tablespoon in the wok. Add the scallions, garlic, chilies, and carrots and stir-fry for about 1 minute. Add the sugar, vinegar, soy sauce, and stock or water, blend well, and then bring to a boil.

5 Stir in the cornstarch paste and simmer for a few minutes to thicken the sauce. Return the beef to the wok and stir until the shreds of meat are well coated with the sauce. Serve hot.

Step *1*

Step *3*

Step *4*

Lamb & Ginger Stir-Fry

*Tenderloin of lamb (or beef or pork) is cooked with garlic, ginger, and
shiitake mushrooms. Serve with noodles or plain boiled rice if preferred.*

SERVES 4

INGREDIENTS

1 lb lamb tenderloin, or
beef or pork
2 tbsp sunflower oil
1 tbsp chopped ginger root
2 garlic cloves, chopped
6 scallions, white and green parts
diagonally sliced
8 oz shiitake mushrooms, sliced
6 oz snow peas
1 tsp cornstarch
2 tbsp dry sherry
1 tbsp light soy sauce
1 tsp sesame oil
1 tbsp sesame seeds, toasted
Chinese egg noodles, to serve

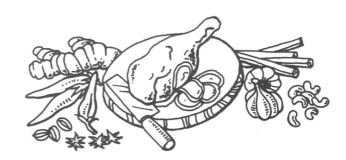

1 Cut the lamb into ¼ in. thick rounds using a very sharp knife.

2 Heat the oil in a wok or skillet. Add the lamb and stir-fry for 2 minutes.

3 Add the ginger, garlic, scallions, mushrooms, and snow peas and stir-fry for a further 2 minutes.

4 Mix the cornstarch with the sherry, add to the wok with the soy sauce and sesame oil, and cook, stirring, for 1 minute until thickened. Sprinkle over the sesame seeds and serve with Chinese egg noodles.

Step *1*

Step *3*

Step *4*

Five-Spice Lamb

Chinese five-spice powder is a blend of cinnamon, fennel, star anise, ginger, and cloves. It gives an authentic Chinese flavor to many dishes.

SERVES 4

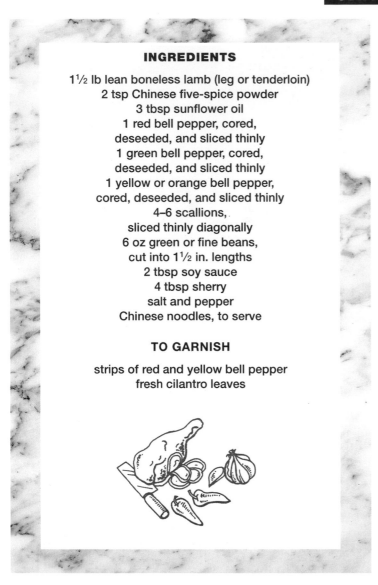

INGREDIENTS

1½ lb lean boneless lamb (leg or tenderloin)
2 tsp Chinese five-spice powder
3 tbsp sunflower oil
1 red bell pepper, cored,
deseeded, and sliced thinly
1 green bell pepper, cored,
deseeded, and sliced thinly
1 yellow or orange bell pepper,
cored, deseeded, and sliced thinly
4–6 scallions,
sliced thinly diagonally
6 oz green or fine beans,
cut into 1½ in. lengths
2 tbsp soy sauce
4 tbsp sherry
salt and pepper
Chinese noodles, to serve

TO GARNISH

strips of red and yellow bell pepper
fresh cilantro leaves

1 Cut the lamb into narrow strips, about 1½ inches long, across the grain. Place in a bowl, add the five-spice powder and ¼ teaspoon salt, mix well, and leave to marinate, covered, in a cool place for at least an hour and up to 24 hours.

2 Heat half the oil in the wok, swirling it around until really hot. Add the lamb and stir-fry briskly for 3–4 minutes until almost cooked. Remove from the pan.

3 Add the remaining oil to the wok and when hot add the bell peppers and scallions. Stir-fry for 2–3 minutes, then add the beans, and stir for a minute or so.

4 Add the soy sauce and sherry to the wok and when hot replace the lamb and any juices. Stir-fry for 1–2 minutes until the lamb is really hot again and thoroughly coated in the sauce. Season to taste.

5 Serve with noodles, garnished with strips of red and green bell pepper and fresh cilantro.

Step *2*

Step *3*

Step *4*

Twice-Cooked Pork

Twice-cooked is a popular way of cooking meat in China. The meat is first boiled to tenderize it, then cut into strips or slices, and stir-fried.

SERVES 4

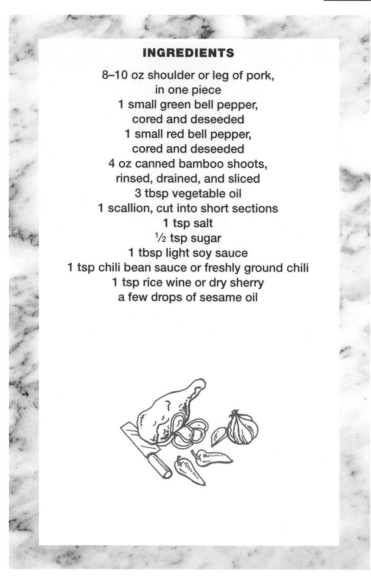

INGREDIENTS

8–10 oz shoulder or leg of pork,
in one piece
1 small green bell pepper,
cored and deseeded
1 small red bell pepper,
cored and deseeded
4 oz canned bamboo shoots,
rinsed, drained, and sliced
3 tbsp vegetable oil
1 scallion, cut into short sections
1 tsp salt
½ tsp sugar
1 tbsp light soy sauce
1 tsp chili bean sauce or freshly ground chili
1 tsp rice wine or dry sherry
a few drops of sesame oil

1 Immerse the pork in a pot of boiling water to cover. Return to a boil and skim the surface. Reduce the heat, cover, and simmer for 15–20 minutes. Turn off the heat and leave the pork in the water to cool for at least 2–3 hours.

2 Remove the pork from the water and drain well. Trim off any excess fat, then cut into small, thin slices. Cut the green and red bell peppers into pieces about the same size as the pork and the sliced bamboo shoots.

3 Heat the oil in a preheated wok and add the bell peppers, bamboo shoots, and scallion. Stir-fry for about 1 minute.

4 Add the pork, followed by the salt, sugar, soy sauce, chili bean sauce, and wine. Blend well, continue stirring for another minute, then sprinkle with sesame oil and serve.

Step *1*

Step *2*

Step *4*

Ribs with Chili

For best results, chop the ribs into small bite-size pieces.

SERVES 4

INGREDIENTS

1 lb pork sparerib
1 tsp sugar
1 tbsp light soy sauce
1 tsp rice wine or dry sherry
1 tsp cornstarch
about 2½ cups vegetable oil
1 garlic clove, chopped finely
1 scallion, cut into short sections
1 small green or red chili,
deseeded and sliced thinly
2 tbsp black bean sauce
about ⅔ cup Chinese Stock (page 16)
or water
1 small onion, diced
1 green bell pepper, cored,
deseeded, and diced

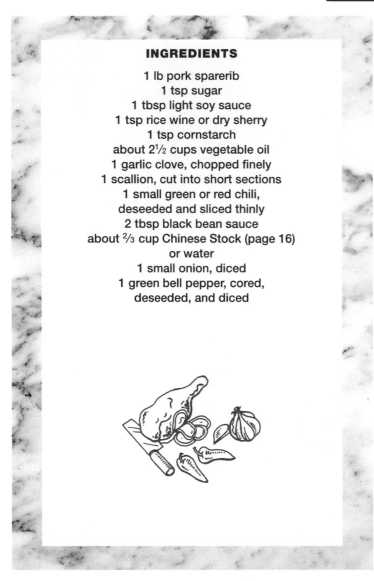

1 Trim the excess fat from the ribs, and chop each one into 3–4 bite-size pieces. Place the ribs in a shallow dish with the sugar, soy sauce, wine, and cornstarch and leave to marinate for 35–45 minutes.

2 Heat the oil in a preheated wok. Add the ribs and deep-fry for 2–3 minutes until light brown. Remove with a perforated spoon and drain on paper towels.

3 Pour off the oil, leaving about 1 tablespoon in the wok. Add the garlic, scallion, chili, and black bean sauce and stir-fry for 30–40 seconds.

4 Add the ribs, blend well, then add the stock or water. Bring to a boil, then reduce the heat, cover, and braise for 8–10 minutes, stirring once or twice.

5 Add the onion and green bell pepper. Increase the heat to high, and stir uncovered for about 2 minutes to reduce the sauce a little. Serve hot.

Step *2*

Step *3*

Step *5*

Fish-Flavored Shredded Pork

*'Fish-flavored' (yu-xiang in Chinese) is a Szechuan cookery term
meaning that the dish contains seasonings normally used in fish dishes.*

SERVES 4

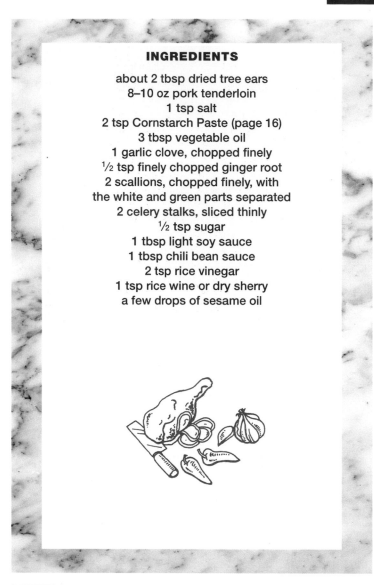

INGREDIENTS

about 2 tbsp dried tree ears
8–10 oz pork tenderloin
1 tsp salt
2 tsp Cornstarch Paste (page 16)
3 tbsp vegetable oil
1 garlic clove, chopped finely
½ tsp finely chopped ginger root
2 scallions, chopped finely, with
the white and green parts separated
2 celery stalks, sliced thinly
½ tsp sugar
1 tbsp light soy sauce
1 tbsp chili bean sauce
2 tsp rice vinegar
1 tsp rice wine or dry sherry
a few drops of sesame oil

1 Soak the tree ears in warm water for about 20 minutes, then rinse in cold water until the water is clear. Drain well, then cut into thin shreds.

2 Cut the pork into thin shreds, then mix in a bowl with a pinch of the salt and about half the cornstarch paste until well coated.

3 Heat 1 tablespoon of oil in a preheated wok. Add the pork strips and stir-fry for about 1 minute, or until the color changes, then remove with a perforated spoon.

4 Add the remaining oil to the wok and heat. Add the garlic, ginger, the white parts of the scallions, the tree ears, and celery. Stir-fry for about 1 minute, then return the pork strips, together with the sugar, soy sauce, chili bean sauce, vinegar, wine, and remaining salt. Blend well and continue stirring for another minute.

5 Finally add the green parts of the scallions and blend in the remaining cornstarch paste and sesame oil. Stir until the sauce has thickened and serve hot.

Step *1*

Step *3*

Step *4*

Braised Pork & Tofu

The pork used in the recipe can be replaced by chicken or shrimp, or it can be omitted altogether.

SERVES 4

INGREDIENTS

3 cakes tofu
4 oz boneless pork
1 leek
1–2 scallions, cut into short sections
a few small dried whole chilies, soaked
vegetable oil for deep-frying
2 tbsp yellow bean sauce
1 tbsp light soy sauce
2 tsp rice wine or dry sherry
a few drops of sesame oil

1 Split each cake of tofu into 3 slices crosswise, then cut each slice diagonally into 2 triangles.

2 Cut the pork into shreds. Cut the leek into thin strips. Drain the chilies, remove the seeds using the tip of a knife, then cut into small shreds.

3 Heat the oil in a preheated wok until smoking, then deep-fry the tofu triangles for 2–3 minutes, or until golden brown all over. Remove with a perforated spoon and drain on paper towels.

4 Pour off the hot oil, leaving about 1 tablespoon in the wok. Add the pork strips, scallions, and chilies and stir-fry for 1 minute or until the pork changes color.

5 Add the leek, tofu, yellow bean sauce, soy sauce, and wine and braise for 2–3 minutes, stirring very gently to blend everything well. Finally sprinkle on the sesame oil and serve.

Step *1*

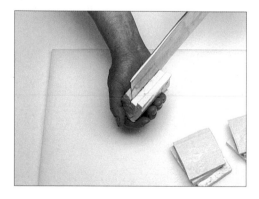

Step *3*

Step *4*

Sweet & Sour Pork

This has to be the most popular Chinese dish all over the world.
To vary, replace pork with fish, shrimp, chicken, or vegetables.

SERVES 4

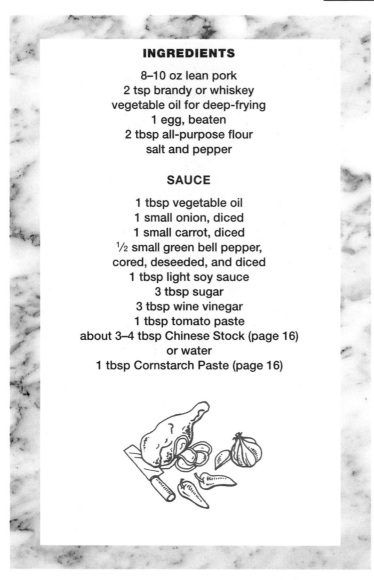

INGREDIENTS

8–10 oz lean pork
2 tsp brandy or whiskey
vegetable oil for deep-frying
1 egg, beaten
2 tbsp all-purpose flour
salt and pepper

SAUCE

1 tbsp vegetable oil
1 small onion, diced
1 small carrot, diced
½ small green bell pepper,
cored, deseeded, and diced
1 tbsp light soy sauce
3 tbsp sugar
3 tbsp wine vinegar
1 tbsp tomato paste
about 3–4 tbsp Chinese Stock (page 16)
or water
1 tbsp Cornstarch Paste (page 16)

1 Cut the pork into small bite-size cubes. Place in a dish with the salt, pepper, and brandy or whiskey and leave to marinate for 15–20 minutes.

2 Heat the oil in a wok or deep-fryer. Place the pork cubes in a bowl with the beaten egg and turn to coat. Sprinkle on the flour and turn the pork cubes until they are well coated.

3 Deep-fry the pork cubes in batches for about 3–4 minutes, stirring gently to separate the pieces. Remove with a perforated spoon and drain on paper towels. Reheat the oil until hot, and return the meat to the wok for another minute or so or until golden brown. Remove the meat with a perforated spoon and drain on paper towels.

4 To make the sauce, heat the oil in a preheated wok, add the vegetables, and stir-fry for about 1 minute. Add the seasonings and tomato paste with the stock or water, bring to a boil, and then thicken with the cornstarch paste.

5 Add the pork and blend well so that each piece of meat is coated with the sauce. Serve hot.

Step *1*

Step *3*

Step *4*

Stir-Fried Pork with Vegetables

This is a basic 'meat and veg' recipe – using pork, chicken, beef, or lamb,
and vegetables according to seasonal availability.

SERVES 4

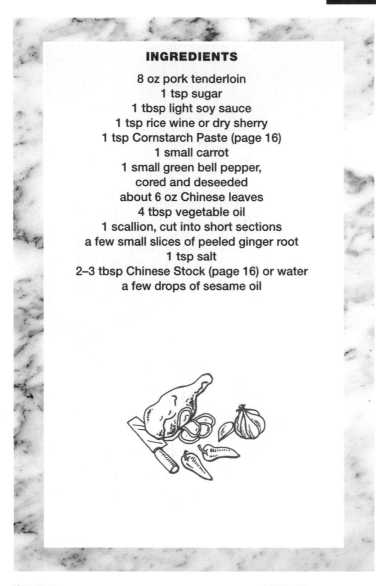

INGREDIENTS

8 oz pork tenderloin
1 tsp sugar
1 tbsp light soy sauce
1 tsp rice wine or dry sherry
1 tsp Cornstarch Paste (page 16)
1 small carrot
1 small green bell pepper,
cored and deseeded
about 6 oz Chinese leaves
4 tbsp vegetable oil
1 scallion, cut into short sections
a few small slices of peeled ginger root
1 tsp salt
2–3 tbsp Chinese Stock (page 16) or water
a few drops of sesame oil

1 Thinly slice the pork tenderloin into small pieces and place in a shallow dish. Add half the sugar, half the the soy sauce, the wine, and cornstarch paste, and leave in the refrigerator to marinate for 10–15 minutes.

2 Cut the carrot, green bell pepper, and Chinese leaves into thin slices roughly the same length and width as the pork pieces.

3 Heat the oil in a preheated wok and stir-fry the pork for about 1 minute to seal in the flavor. Remove with a perforated spoon and keep warm.

4 Add the carrot, bell pepper, Chinese leaves, scallion, and ginger and stir-fry for about 2 minutes.

5 Add the salt and remaining sugar, followed by the pork and remaining soy sauce, and the stock or water. Blend well and stir for another 1–2 minutes until hot. Sprinkle with the sesame oil and serve.

Step *2*

Step *3*

Step *4*

Fish Eggplant & Pork

*Like Fish-Flavored Shredded Pork (page 162),
there is no fish involved in this dish.*

SERVES 4

INGREDIENTS

1 lb eggplant
vegetable oil for deep-frying
1 garlic clove, chopped finely
½ tsp finely chopped ginger root
2 scallions, chopped finely,
with the white and green parts separated
6 oz pork, shredded thinly
1 tbsp light soy sauce
2 tsp rice wine or dry sherry
1 tbsp chili bean sauce
½ tsp salt
½ tsp sugar
1 tbsp rice vinegar
2 tsp Cornstarch Paste (page 16)
a few drops of sesame oil

1 Cut the eggplant into rounds and then into thin strips about the size of French fries – the skin can either be peeled or left on.

2 Heat the oil in a preheated wok until smoking. Add the eggplant strips and deep-fry for about 3–4 minutes, or until soft. Remove and drain thoroughly on paper towels.

3 Pour off the hot oil, leaving about 1 tablespoon in the wok. Add the garlic, ginger, and the white parts of the scallions, followed by the pork (if using). Stir-fry for about 1 minute or until the color of the meat changes, then add the soy sauce, wine, and chili bean sauce, blending well.

4 Return the eggplant strips to the wok and add the salt, sugar, and vinegar. Continue stirring for another minute or so, then add the cornstarch paste, and stir until the sauce has thickened.

5 Add the green parts of the scallions and sprinkle on the sesame oil. Serve hot.

Step 2

Step 3

Step 4

VEGETABLE DISHES

Being basically an agricultural country, China has really perfected vegetable cooking to a fine art. The stir-frying technique, in which ingredients are quickly cooked over high heat in a minimum of oil or water, ensures that flavor, texture, and color are preserved, as well as valuable nutrients.

The Chinese eat far more vegetables than meat or poultry, and with few exceptions, almost all meat and poultry dishes include some kind of vegetable as a supplementary ingredient – the idea being to give the dish a harmonious balance of color, aroma, flavor, and texture.

When selecting vegetables for cooking, the Chinese attach great importance to quality. Chinese cooks visit the market on a daily basis to buy fresh produce for the family meal. When selecting vegetables for a Chinese meal, always buy crisp, firm specimens, and cook them as soon as possible.

Another point to remember is to wash the vegetables just before cutting, in order to avoid losing vitamins in water. They should also be cooked immediately after being cut so that the vitamin content is not lost through evaporation.

Sweet & Sour Vegetables

Make your choice of vegetables from the suggested list, including scallions and garlic. For a hotter, spicier sauce add chili sauce.

SERVES 4

INGREDIENTS

5–6 vegetables from the following:
1 bell pepper, deseeded and sliced
4 oz green beans, cut into 2–3 pieces
4 oz snow peas,
cut into 2–3 pieces
8 oz broccoli or cauliflower flowerets
8 oz zucchini,
cut into 2 in. lengths
6 oz carrots, cut into julienne strips
4 oz baby corncobs, sliced thinly
6 oz parsnip or celery root, diced finely
13 celery sticks, sliced thinly crosswise
4 tomatoes, skinned, quartered, and deseeded
4 oz button mushrooms, sliced
3 in. length of cucumber, diced
7 oz can water chestnuts or
bamboo shoots, drained and sliced
14 oz can bean-sprouts, drained
4 scallions sliced thinly
1 garlic clove, crushed
2 tbsp sunflower oil

SWEET & SOUR SAUCE

2 tbsp wine vinegar
2 tbsp clear honey
1 tbsp tomato paste
2 tbsp soy sauce
2 tbsp sherry
1–2 tsp sweet chili sauce (optional)
2 tsp cornstarch

1 Prepare the selected vegetables, cutting them into uniform lengths.

2 Combine the sauce ingredients in a bowl, blending well together.

3 Heat the oil in the wok, swirling it around until really hot. Add the scallions and garlic and stir-fry for 1 minute.

4 Add the prepared vegetables – the harder and firmer ones first – and stir-fry for 2 minutes. Then add the softer ones, such as mushrooms, snow peas, and tomatoes, and continue to stir-fry for 2 minutes.

5 Add the sweet and sour mixture to the wok. Bring to a boil quickly, tossing until the vegetables are thoroughly coated and the sauce has thickened. Serve hot.

Step *1*

Step *2*

Step *5*

Stir-Fried Mixed Vegetables

*The Chinese never mix ingredients indiscriminately – they are carefully
selected to achieve a harmonious balance of colors and textures.*

SERVES 4

INGREDIENTS

2 oz snow peas
1 small carrot
4 oz Chinese leaves
4 oz fresh bean-sprouts
2 oz black or white mushrooms
2 oz canned bamboo shoots, rinsed
and drained
3–4 tbsp vegetable oil
1 tsp salt
1 tsp sugar
1 tbsp oyster sauce or light soy sauce
a few drops of sesame oil (optional)
dip sauce, to serve (optional)

1 Prepare the vegetables: top and tail the snow peas, and cut the carrot, Chinese leaves, mushrooms, and bamboo shoots into roughly the same shape and size as the snow peas.

2 Heat the oil in a preheated wok, and add the carrot first. Stir-fry for a few seconds, then add the snow peas and Chinese leaves, and stir-fry for about 1 minute.

3 Add the bean-sprouts, mushrooms, and bamboo shoots and stir-fry for another minute.

4 Add the salt and sugar, continue stirring for another minute, then add the oyster sauce or soy sauce. Blend well, and sprinkle with sesame oil (if using). Serve hot or cold, with a dip sauce, if liked.

Step *1*

Step *2*

Step *4*

Stir-Fried Seasonal Vegetables

When selecting different fresh vegetables for this dish, bear in mind that
there should always be a contrast in color as well as texture.

SERVES 4

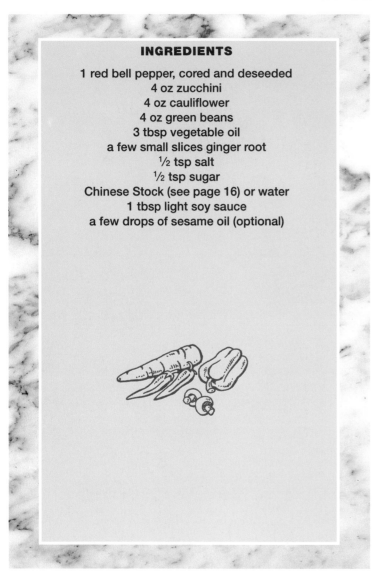

INGREDIENTS

1 red bell pepper, cored and deseeded
4 oz zucchini
4 oz cauliflower
4 oz green beans
3 tbsp vegetable oil
a few small slices ginger root
½ tsp salt
½ tsp sugar
Chinese Stock (see page 16) or water
1 tbsp light soy sauce
a few drops of sesame oil (optional)

1 Cut the red bell pepper into small squares. Thinly slice the zucchini. Trim the cauliflower and divide into small flowerets, discarding any thick stems. Make sure the vegetables are cut into roughly similar shapes and sizes to ensure even cooking. Top and tail the green beans, then cut them in half.

2 Heat the oil in a preheated wok, add the vegetables, and stir-fry with the ginger for about 2 minutes.

3 Add the salt and sugar, and continue to stir-fry for 1–2 minutes, adding a little Chinese stock or water if the vegetables appear to be too dry. Do not add liquid unless it seems necessary.

4 Add the soy sauce and sesame oil (if using). Blend well to lightly coat the vegetables. Serve immediately.

Step *1*

Step *1*

Step *3*

Vegetable & Nut Stir-Fry

A colorful selection of vegetables are stir-fried in a creamy peanut sauce and sprinkled with nuts to serve.

SERVES 4

INGREDIENTS

3 tbsp crunchy peanut butter
⅔ cup water
1 tbsp soy sauce
1 tsp sugar
1 carrot
½ red onion
4 baby zucchini
1 red bell pepper
8 oz egg thread noodles
¼ cup peanuts, chopped roughly
2 tbsp vegetable oil
1 tsp sesame oil
1 small green chili, deseeded and sliced thinly
1 garlic clove, sliced thinly
7 oz can water chestnuts,
drained and sliced
3 cups bean-sprouts
salt

1 In a small bowl, gradually blend the peanut butter with the water. Stir in the soy sauce and sugar.

2 Cut the carrot into thin matchsticks and slice the onion. Slice the zucchini on the diagonal, and cut the bell pepper into chunks.

3 Bring a large pan of water to a boil and add the egg noodles. Remove from the heat immediately and leave to rest for 4 minutes, stirring occasionally to divide the noodles.

4 Heat a wok or large skillet, add the peanuts, and dry-fry until they are beginning to brown. Remove and set aside.

5 Add the oils to the wok or skillet and heat. Add the carrot, onion, zucchini, bell pepper, chili, and garlic, and stir-fry for 2–3 minutes. Add the water chestnuts, bean-sprouts, and peanut sauce. Bring to a boil and heat thoroughly. Season to taste. Drain the noodles and serve with the stir-fry. Sprinkle with the peanuts.

Step *1*

Step *3*

Step *5*

Ma-Po Tofu

Ma-Po, the wife of a Szechuan chef, created this dish in the 19th century.
Replace the beef with dried mushrooms to make a vegetarian meal.

SERVES 4

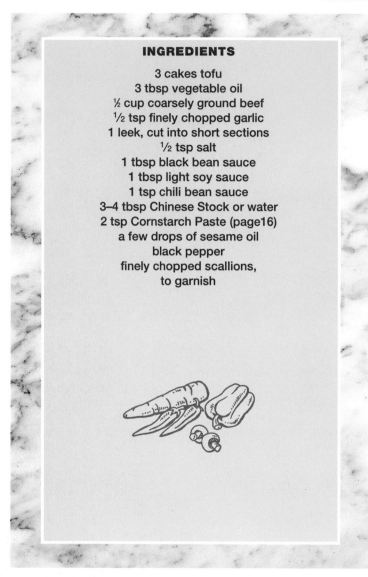

INGREDIENTS

3 cakes tofu
3 tbsp vegetable oil
½ cup coarsely ground beef
½ tsp finely chopped garlic
1 leek, cut into short sections
½ tsp salt
1 tbsp black bean sauce
1 tbsp light soy sauce
1 tsp chili bean sauce
3–4 tbsp Chinese Stock or water
2 tsp Cornstarch Paste (page16)
a few drops of sesame oil
black pepper
finely chopped scallions,
to garnish

1 Cut the tofu into ½ in. cubes, handling it carefully. Bring some water to a boil in a small pan or a wok, add the tofu, and blanch for 2–3 minutes to harden. Remove and drain well.

2 Heat the oil in a preheated wok. Add the ground beef and garlic and stir-fry for about 1 minute, or until the color of the beef changes. Add the leek, salt, and sauces and blend well.

3 Add the stock or water and the tofu. Bring to a boil and braise gently for 2–3 minutes.

4 Add the cornstarch paste, and stir until the sauce has thickened. Sprinkle with sesame oil and black pepper, and garnish with scallions.

Step *1*

Step *2*

Step *4*

Tofu & Vegetables with Black Bean Sauce

Chunks of tofu are stir-fried with vegetables and black bean sauce. The recipe can be stir-fried in a wok or cooked in a microwave.

SERVES 4

INGREDIENTS

9½ oz smoked tofu, cubed
2 tbsp soy sauce
1 tbsp dry sherry
1 tsp sesame oil
4 dried Chinese mushrooms,
soaked in warm water for 30 minutes
2 tbsp groundnut oil
1 carrot, cut into thin sticks
1 celery stalk, cut into thin sticks
4 oz (16–18) baby corncobs,
halved lengthwise
1 zucchini, sliced
4 scallions, chopped
1⅓ cups snow peas,
each cut into 3 pieces
2 tbsp black bean sauce
1 tsp cornstarch
salt and pepper
1 tbsp toasted sesame seeds, to garnish
egg noodles, to serve

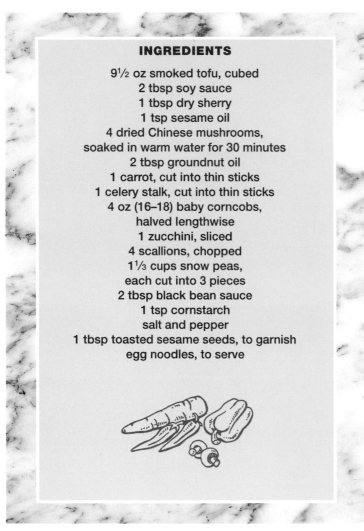

1 Marinate the tofu in the soy sauce, sherry, and sesame oil for 30 minutes.

2 Drain the mushrooms, reserving 1 tablespoon of the liquid. Squeeze out excess water from the mushrooms and discard the hard centers. Thinly slice the mushrooms.

3 Heat the groundnut oil in a wok until very hot. Add the carrot, celery, and corncobs and stir-fry for 2 minutes. Alternatively, place in a large bowl, cover, and microwave on HIGH power for 1 minute.

4 Add the mushrooms, zucchini, scallions, and snow peas. Stir-fry for 4–5 minutes until just tender. Alternatively, cover and microwave on HIGH power for 4 minutes, stirring every minute.

5 Add the black bean sauce. Mix the cornstarch with the reserved mushroom water and stir into the vegetables, with the tofu and marinade. Stir-fry, or cover and microwave on HIGH power for 2–3 minutes until heated through and the sauce has thickened slightly. Season to taste. Garnish the vegetables with sesame seeds and serve with the noodles.

Step *1*

Step *2*

Step *4*

Vegetable & Tofu Casserole

This colorful Chinese-style casserole is made with tofu, vegetables, and black bean sauce.

SERVES 4

INGREDIENTS

6 Chinese dried mushrooms
(or thinly sliced open-cup mushrooms)
9 oz tofu
3 tbsp vegetable oil
1 carrot, cut into thin strips
4 oz snow peas
8 baby corncobs, halved lengthwise
7½ oz can bamboo shoots,
drained and sliced
1 red bell pepper, cored, deseeded, and
cut into chunks
1½ cups Chinese leaves, shredded
1 tbsp soy sauce
1 tbsp black bean sauce
1 tsp sugar
1 tsp cornstarch
vegetable oil for deep-frying
8 oz Chinese rice noodles
salt

1 Place the dried mushrooms in a small bowl and cover with warm water. Leave to soak for 20–25 minutes. Drain and squeeze out the excess water, reserving the liquid. Remove the tough centers and slice the mushrooms thinly.

2 Cut the tofu into cubes. Boil in a saucepan of lightly salted water for 2–3 minutes to firm up. Drain thoroughly.

3 Heat half the oil in a large flameproof casserole or saucepan. Add the tofu and fry until lightly browned all over. Remove with a perforated spoon and drain on paper towels.

4 Add the remaining oil and stir-fry the mushrooms, carrot, snow peas, corncobs, bamboo shoots, and bell pepper for 2–3 minutes. Add the Chinese leaves and tofu, and stir-fry for a further 2 minutes.

5 Stir in the soy sauce, black bean sauce, and sugar, and season with salt. Add 6 tablespoons of the reserved mushroom liquid (or water if you are using ordinary mushrooms), mixed with cornstarch. Bring to a boil, reduce the heat, cover, and braise for 2–3 minutes until the sauce has thickened slightly.

6 Heat the oil for deep-frying in a large saucepan. Add the noodles in batches and deep-fry until puffed up and lightly golden. Drain on paper towels and serve with the casserole.

Step *3*

Step *4*

Step *6*

Stir-Fried Mushrooms, Cucumber, & Smoked Tofu

Chunks of cucumber and smoked tofu stir-fried with straw mushrooms,
snow peas, and corn in a yellow bean sauce.

SERVES 4

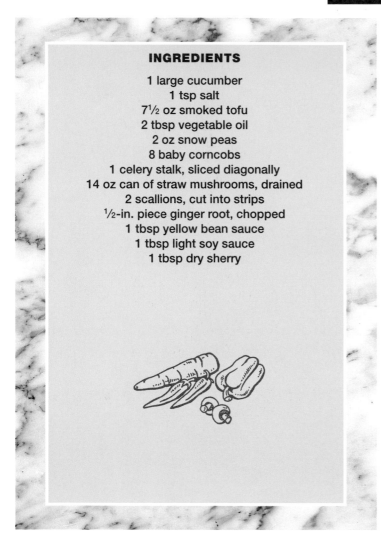

INGREDIENTS

1 large cucumber
1 tsp salt
7½ oz smoked tofu
2 tbsp vegetable oil
2 oz snow peas
8 baby corncobs
1 celery stalk, sliced diagonally
14 oz can of straw mushrooms, drained
2 scallions, cut into strips
½-in. piece ginger root, chopped
1 tbsp yellow bean sauce
1 tbsp light soy sauce
1 tbsp dry sherry

1 Halve the cucumber lengthwise. Remove the seeds, using a teaspoon. Cut into cubes, place in a colander, and sprinkle over the salt. Leave to drain for 10 minutes. Rinse thoroughly in cold water to remove the salt and drain thoroughly.

2 Cut the tofu into cubes. Heat the oil in a wok or large skillet. Add the tofu, snow peas, corncobs, and celery. Stir until the tofu is lightly browned.

3 Add the straw mushrooms, scallions, and ginger, and stir-fry for a further minute.

4 Stir in the cucumber, yellow bean sauce, soy sauce, sherry, and 2 tablespoons of water.

5 Stir-fry for 1 minute before serving.

Step *1*	Step *2*	Step *4*

Money Bags

These steamed dumplings are filled with mushroom and corn. Try dipping them in a mixture of soy sauce, sherry, and slivers of ginger root.

SERVES 4

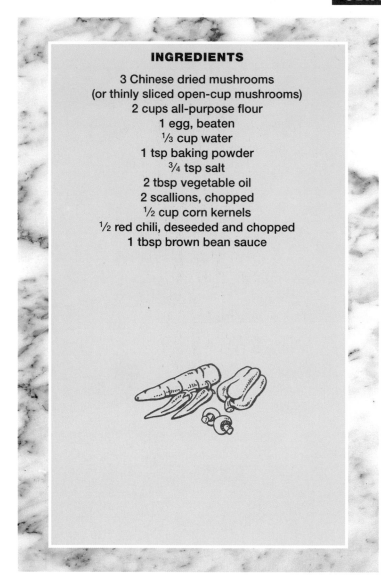

INGREDIENTS

3 Chinese dried mushrooms
(or thinly sliced open-cup mushrooms)
2 cups all-purpose flour
1 egg, beaten
⅓ cup water
1 tsp baking powder
¾ tsp salt
2 tbsp vegetable oil
2 scallions, chopped
½ cup corn kernels
½ red chili, deseeded and chopped
1 tbsp brown bean sauce

1 Place the dried mushrooms in a small bowl, cover with warm water, and leave to soak for 20–25 minutes.

2 To make the wrappers, sift the flour into a bowl. Add the egg and mix lightly. Stir in the water, baking powder, and salt. Mix to a soft dough. Knead lightly until smooth on a floured board. Cover with a damp cloth and set aside for 5–6 minutes. This allows the baking powder time to activate, so that the dumplings swell when they are steamed.

3 Drain the mushrooms, squeezing them dry. Remove the tough centers and chop the mushrooms.

4 Heat the oil in a wok or large skillet and stir-fry the mushrooms, scallions, corn, and chili for 2 minutes. Stir in the brown bean sauce and remove from the heat.

5 Roll the dough into a large sausage and cut into 24 even-size pieces.

6 Roll each piece out into a thin round and place a teaspoonful of the filling in the center. Gather up the edges, pinch together, and twist to seal.

7 Stand the dumplings in an oiled steaming basket. Place over a saucepan of simmering water, cover, and steam for 12–14 minutes before serving.

Step *2*

Step *6*

Step *7*

Lentil Balls with Sweet & Sour Sauce

Crisp golden lentil balls are served in a sweet and sour sauce with bell peppers and pineapple chunks.

SERVES 4

INGREDIENTS

1 cup red lentils
scant 2 cups water
½ green chili, deseeded and chopped
4 scallions, chopped finely
1 garlic clove, crushed
1 tsp salt
4 tbsp pineapple juice from can
1 egg, beaten
vegetable oil for deep-frying
rice or noodles, to serve

SAUCE

3 tbsp white wine vinegar
2 tbsp sugar
2 tbsp tomato paste
1 tsp sesame oil
1 tsp cornstarch
½ tsp salt
6 tbsp water
2 canned pineapple rings
2 tbsp vegetable oil
½ red bell pepper, deseeded and
cut into chunks
½ green bell pepper, deseeded and
cut into chunks

1 Wash the lentils, then put them in a saucepan with the water, and bring to a boil. Skim and boil rapidly for 10 minutes, uncovered. Reduce the heat and simmer for 5 minutes until you have a dry mixture. Considerably less water is used to cook these lentils than is normally required, so take care they do not burn as they cook. Stir occasionally.

2 Remove the lentils from the heat and stir in the chili, scallions, garlic, salt, and pineapple juice. Leave to cool for 10 minutes.

3 To make the sauce, mix together the vinegar, sugar, tomato paste, sesame oil, cornstarch, salt, and water, and set aside. Cut the pineapple into chunks.

4 Add the beaten egg to the lentil mixture. Heat the oil in a large saucepan or wok and deep-fry tablespoonfuls of the mixture in batches until crisp and golden. Remove with a perforated spoon and drain on paper towels.

5 Heat the 2 tablespoons oil in a wok or skillet. Stir-fry the bell peppers for 2 minutes. Add the sauce mixture with the pineapple chunks. Bring to a boil, then reduce the heat, and simmer for 1 minute, stirring constantly, until the sauce has thickened. Add the lentil balls and heat thoroughly, taking care not to break them up. Serve with rice or noodles.

Step *1*

Step *4*

Step *5*

Eggplant in Chili Sauce

*Strips of eggplant are deep-fried, then served in a fragrant chili sauce
with carrot matchsticks and scallions.*

SERVES 4

INGREDIENTS

1 large eggplant
vegetable oil for deep-frying
2 carrots
4 scallions
2 large garlic cloves
1 tbsp vegetable oil
2 tsp chili sauce
1 tbsp soy sauce
1 tbsp dry sherry

1 Slice the eggplant and then cut into strips about the size of French fries.

2 Heat enough oil in a large heavy-based saucepan to deep-fry the eggplant in batches until just browned. Remove the strips with a perforated spoon and drain on paper towels.

3 Cut the carrots into thin matchsticks. Trim and slice the scallions diagonally. Slice the garlic cloves thinly.

4 Heat 1 tablespoon of oil in a wok or large skillet. Add the carrot matchsticks and stir-fry for 1 minute. Add the chopped scallions and garlic, and stir-fry for a further minute.

5 Stir in the chili sauce, soy sauce, and sherry, then stir in the drained eggplant. Stir well until the vegetables are thoroughly heated through before serving.

Step *1*

Step *2*

Step *5*

Eggplant in Black Bean Sauce

*Stir-fried eggplant is served in a black bean sauce with garlic and
scallions. Serve with with rice.*

SERVES 4

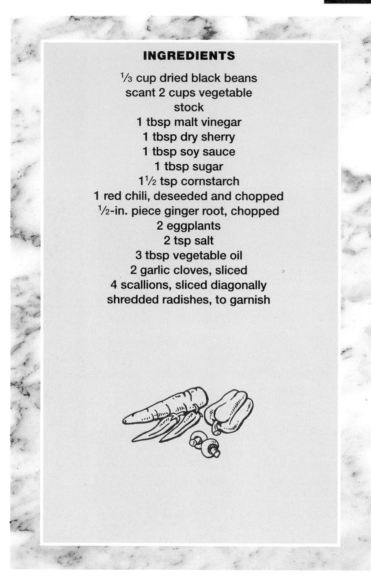

INGREDIENTS

⅓ cup dried black beans
scant 2 cups vegetable
stock
1 tbsp malt vinegar
1 tbsp dry sherry
1 tbsp soy sauce
1 tbsp sugar
1½ tsp cornstarch
1 red chili, deseeded and chopped
½-in. piece ginger root, chopped
2 eggplants
2 tsp salt
3 tbsp vegetable oil
2 garlic cloves, sliced
4 scallions, sliced diagonally
shredded radishes, to garnish

1 Soak the beans overnight in plenty of cold water. Drain and place in a saucepan. Cover with cold water, bring to a boil, and boil rapidly, uncovered, for 10 minutes. Drain. Return the beans to the saucepan with the stock and bring to a boil.

2 Blend together the vinegar, sherry, soy sauce, sugar, cornstarch, chili, and ginger in a small bowl. Add to the beans, then cover, and simmer for 40 minutes, or until the beans are tender and the sauce has thickened. Stir occasionally.

3 Cut the eggplants into chunks and place in a colander. Sprinkle with the salt and leave to drain for 30 minutes. Rinse well to remove the salt and dry on paper towels.

4 Heat the oil in a wok or large skillet. Add the eggplant and garlic. Stir-fry for 3–4 minutes until the eggplant has started to brown.

5 Add the sauce to the eggplant with the scallions. Heat thoroughly and garnish with radish shreds.

Step *2*

Step *3*

Step *4*

Gingered Broccoli with Orange

*Thinly sliced broccoli flowerets are lightly stir-fried and
served in a ginger and orange sauce.*

SERVES 4

INGREDIENTS

1½ lb broccoli
2 thin slices ginger root
2 garlic cloves
1 orange
2 tsp cornstarch
1 tbsp light soy sauce
½ tsp sugar
2 tbsp vegetable oil

1 Divide the broccoli into small flowerets. Peel the stems, using a vegetable peeler, and then cut the stems into thin slices. Cut the ginger root into matchsticks and slice the garlic.

2 Peel 2 long strips of zest from the orange and cut into thin strips. Place the strips in a bowl, cover with cold water, and set aside. Squeeze the juice from the orange and mix with the cornstarch, soy sauce, sugar, and 4 tablespoons water.

3 Heat the oil in a wok or large skillet. Add the sliced broccoli stems and stir-fry for 2 minutes. Add the ginger root, garlic, and broccoli flowerets, and stir-fry for a further 3 minutes.

4 Stir in the orange sauce mixture and cook, stirring constantly, until the sauce has thickened and coated the broccoli.

5 Drain the reserved orange rind and stir in before serving.

Step *1*

Step *2*

Step *3*

Broccoli in Oyster Sauce

Some Cantonese restaurants use only the stalks of the broccoli for this dish, for the crunchy texture.

SERVES 4

INGREDIENTS

8–10 oz broccoli
3 tbsp vegetable oil
3–4 small slices ginger root
½ tsp salt
½ tsp sugar
3–4 tbsp Chinese Stock
(page 16) or water
1 tbsp oyster sauce

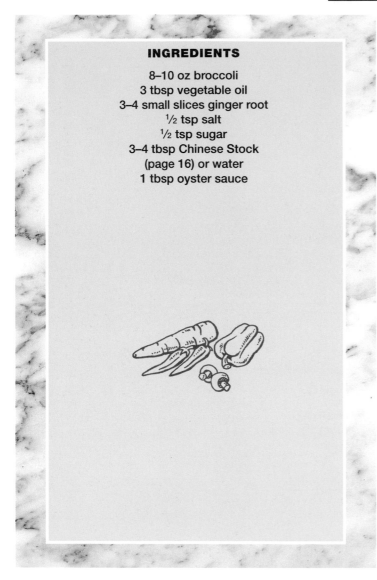

1 Cut the broccoli spears into small flowerets. Trim the stalks, peel off the rough skin, and cut the stalks diagonally into diamond-shaped chunks.

2 Heat the oil in a preheated wok and add the pieces of stalk and the ginger. Stir-fry for half a minute, then add the flowerets, and continue to stir-fry for another 2 minutes.

3 Add the salt, sugar, and stock or water, and continue stirring for another minute or so.

4 Blend in the oyster sauce. Serve hot or cold.

Step *1*

Step *3*

Step *4*

Spinach with Straw Mushrooms

Straw mushrooms (available in cans from oriental shops) are served with spinach, raisins, and pine nuts.

SERVES 4

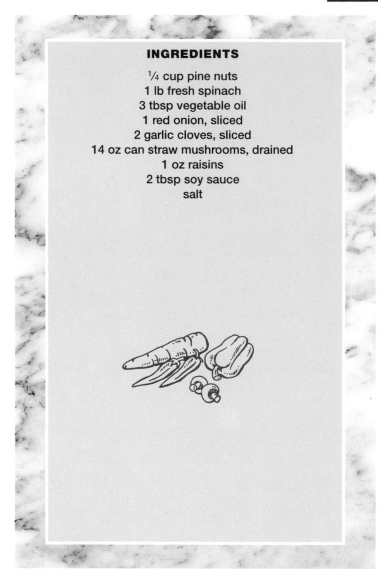

INGREDIENTS

¼ cup pine nuts
1 lb fresh spinach
3 tbsp vegetable oil
1 red onion, sliced
2 garlic cloves, sliced
14 oz can straw mushrooms, drained
1 oz raisins
2 tbsp soy sauce
salt

1 Heat a wok or large skillet and dry-fry the pine nuts until lightly browned. Remove and set aside.

2 Wash the spinach thoroughly, picking the leaves over and removing long stalks. Drain and pat dry with paper towels.

3 Heat the oil in the wok or skillet. Add the onion and garlic, and stir-fry for 1 minute.

4 Add the spinach and mushrooms, and stir-fry until the leaves have wilted. Drain any excess liquid.

5 Stir in the raisins, reserved pine nuts, and soy sauce. Stir-fry until thoroughly heated and well mixed. Season with salt to taste before serving.

Step *1*

Step *4*

Step *5*

Stir-Fried Bean-Sprouts

Be sure to use fresh bean-sprouts, rather than the canned variety, for this crunchy-textured dish.

SERVES 4

INGREDIENTS

8 oz fresh bean-sprouts
2–3 scallions
1 red chili (optional)
3 tbsp vegetable oil
½ tsp salt
½ tsp sugar
1 tbsp light soy sauce
a few drops of sesame oil (optional)

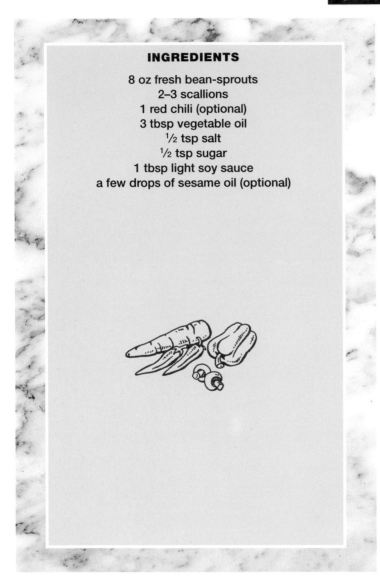

1 Rinse the bean-sprouts in cold water, discarding any husks or small pieces that float to the top. Drain well on paper towels.

2 Cut the scallions into short sections. Shred the chili, if using, discarding the seeds.

3 Heat the oil in a preheated wok. Add the bean-sprouts, scallions, and chili, if using, and stir-fry for about 2 minutes.

4 Add the salt, sugar, soy sauce, and sesame oil, if using. Stir well to blend. Serve hot or cold.

Step *1*

Step *2*

Step *3*

Golden Needles with Bamboo Shoots

Golden needles are the dried flower buds of the tiger lily. Sold in dried form at specialty Chinese shops, they give a unique musky flavor.

SERVES 4

INGREDIENTS

¼ cup dried tiger lily buds
2 × 7½ oz cans bamboo shoots, drained
½ cup cornstarch
vegetable oil for deep-frying
1 tbsp vegetable oil
scant 2 cups vegetable stock
1 tbsp dark soy sauce
1 tbsp dry sherry
1 tsp sugar
1 large garlic clove, sliced
½ each red, green, and yellow bell peppers,
deseeded and sliced thinly

1 Soak the tiger lily buds in hot water for 30 minutes.

2 Coat the bamboo shoots in cornstarch. Heat the oil for deep-frying in a large heavy-based saucepan. Deep-fry the bamboo shoots in batches until just beginning to color. Remove with a perforated spoon and drain on paper towels.

3 Drain the tiger lily buds and trim off the hard ends. Heat 1 tablespoon oil in a wok or large skillet. Add the tiger lily buds, bamboo shoots, stock, soy sauce, sherry, sugar, and garlic.

4 Add the bell pepper to the wok or skillet. Bring to a boil, stirring constantly, then reduce the heat, and simmer for 5 minutes. Add extra water or stock if necessary.

Step *1*

Step *3*

Step *4*

Braised Chinese Leaves

White cabbage can be used instead of the Chinese leaves for this dish.

SERVES 4

INGREDIENTS

1 lb Chinese leaves or firm
white cabbage
3 tbsp vegetable oil
½ tsp Szechuan peppercorns
5–6 small dried red chilies, deseeded and chopped
½ tsp salt
1 tbsp sugar
1 tbsp light soy sauce
1 tbsp rice vinegar
a few drops of sesame oil (optional)

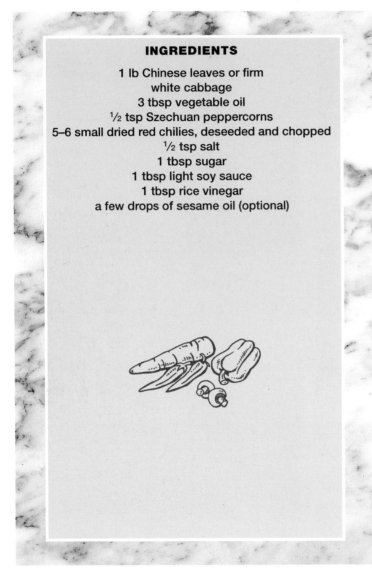

1 Shred the Chinese leaves or cabbage crosswise into thin pieces. (If using firm-packed white cabbage, cut out the thick core before shredding.)

2 Heat the oil in a preheated wok, add the Szechuan peppercorns and the dried chilies, and stir-fry for a few seconds.

3 Add the Chinese leaves or white cabbage to the peppercorns and chilies, stir-fry for about 1 minute, then add salt, and continue stirring for another minute.

4 Add the sugar, soy sauce, and vinegar, blend well, and stir-fry for one more minute. Sprinkle with the sesame oil, if using. Serve hot or cold.

Step *1*

Step *2*

Step *4*

Lemon Chinese Leaves

These stir-fried Chinese leaves are served with a tangy sauce made of grated lemon rind, lemon juice, and ginger.

SERVES 4

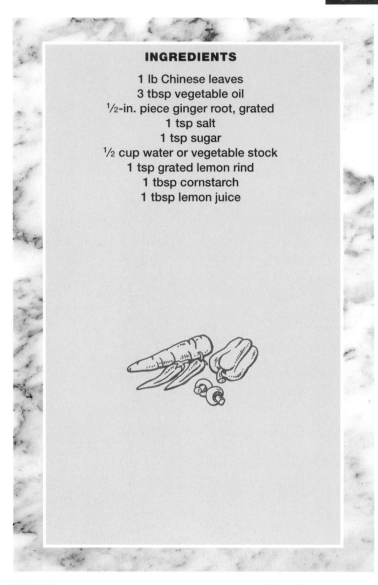

INGREDIENTS

1 lb Chinese leaves
3 tbsp vegetable oil
½-in. piece ginger root, grated
1 tsp salt
1 tsp sugar
½ cup water or vegetable stock
1 tsp grated lemon rind
1 tbsp cornstarch
1 tbsp lemon juice

1 Separate the Chinese leaves, wash, and drain thoroughly. Pat dry with paper towels. Cut into 2 in. wide slices.

2 Heat the oil in a wok or large skillet. Add the grated ginger root, followed by the Chinese leaves, and stir-fry for 2–3 minutes or until the leaves begin to wilt. Add the salt and sugar, and mix well until the leaves soften. Remove the leaves with a perforated spoon and set aside.

3 Add the water or vegetable stock to the wok or skillet with the grated lemon zest, and bring to a boil. Meanwhile, mix the cornstarch to a smooth paste with the lemon juice, then add to the water or stock in the wok or skillet. Simmer, stirring constantly, for about 1 minute to make a smooth sauce.

4 Return the cooked leaves to the wok or skillet and mix thoroughly. Arrange on a serving plate and serve immediately.

Step *1*

Step *3*

Step *4*

Chinese Braised Vegetables

This colorful selection of braised vegetables makes a splendid accompaniment to a main dish.

SERVES 4–6

INGREDIENTS

3 tbsp sunflower oil
1 garlic clove, crushed
1 head Chinese leaves, shredded thickly
2 onions, cut into wedges
8 oz broccoli flowerets
2 large carrots, cut into julienne strips
12 baby corncobs, halved if large
2 oz snow peas, halved
3 oz Chinese or oyster mushrooms, sliced
1 tbsp grated ginger root
1¾ cup vegetable stock
2 tbsp light soy sauce
1 tbsp cornstarch
salt and pepper
½ tsp sugar

1 Heat the oil in a large, heavy-based skillet or wok. Add the garlic, Chinese leaves, onions, broccoli, carrots, corn, snow peas, mushrooms, and ginger and stir-fry for 2 minutes.

2 Add the stock, cover, and cook for a further 2–3 minutes.

3 Blend the soy sauce with the cornstarch and salt and pepper to taste.

4 Remove the braised vegetables from the skillet or wok with a perforated spoon and keep warm. Add the soy sauce mixture to the pan juices, mixing well. Bring to a boil, stirring constantly, until the mixture thickens slightly. Stir in the sugar.

5 Return the vegetables to the skillet or wok and toss in the slightly thickened sauce. Cook gently to just heat through, then serve immediately.

Step *1*

Step *2*

Step *5*

Braised Vegetables with Tofu

Also called Lo Han Zhai or Buddha's Delight, the original recipe uses 18 vegetables to represent the 18 Buddhas (Lo Han) – but 6–8 are acceptable.

SERVES 4

INGREDIENTS

¼ oz dried tree ears
1 cake tofu
2 oz snow peas
4 oz Chinese leaves
1 small carrot
3 oz canned baby corncobs, drained
3 oz canned straw mushrooms, drained
2 oz canned water chestnuts, drained
1¼ cups vegetable oil
1 tsp salt
½ tsp sugar
1 tbsp light soy sauce or oyster sauce
2–3 tbsp Chinese Stock (page 16) or water
a few drops of sesame oil

1 Soak the tree ears in warm water for 15–20 minutes, then rinse, and drain, discarding any hard bits, and dry on paper towels.

2 Cut the cake of tofu into about 18 small pieces. Top and tail the snow peas. Cut the Chinese leaves and the carrot into slices roughly the same size and shape as the snow peas. Cut the baby corncobs, the straw mushrooms, and the water chestnuts in half.

3 Heat the oil in a preheated wok. Add the tofu and deep-fry for about 2 minutes until it turns slightly golden. Remove with a perforated spoon and drain on paper towels.

4 Pour off the oil, leaving about 2 tablespoons in the wok. Add the carrot, Chinese leaves, and snow peas and stir-fry for about 1 minute.

5 Now add the corncobs, mushrooms, and water chestnuts. Stir gently for 2 more minutes, then add the salt, sugar, soy sauce, and stock or water. Bring to a boil and stir-fry for 1 more minute.

6 Sprinkle with sesame oil and serve hot or cold.

Step *1*

Step *2*

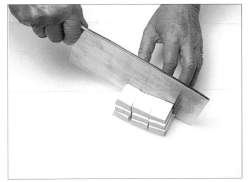

Step *5*

RICE DISHES

Together with noodles, rice forms the central part of
most Chinese meals, particularly in the southern part
of China. In the north, the staple foods tend to be more
wheat-based. Although bland in itself, rice provides a
complementary texture to the other ingredients and
absorbs the stronger flavors of other dishes, making
it an essential and very satisfying part of the
Chinese meal.

For an everyday meal, plain rice is served with two or
three other dishes - usually meat and vegetables,
together with a soup. Rice can be boiled and then
steamed, or it can be fried with other ingredients, such
as scrambled egg, scallions, or peas, then flavored
with soy sauce.

The most common types of rice used in Chinese cuisine
include white or brown long-grain rice and glutinous
rice. The shorter grain of the glutinous rice has a slight
stickiness when cooked, which makes it ideal for eating
with chopsticks. Rice is also used to make wines,
vinegars, noodles, and flour.

Chinese Fried Rice

The rice for this dish may be cooked in the wok or in a saucepan, but it is essential to use cold, dry rice with separate grains for success.

SERVES 4

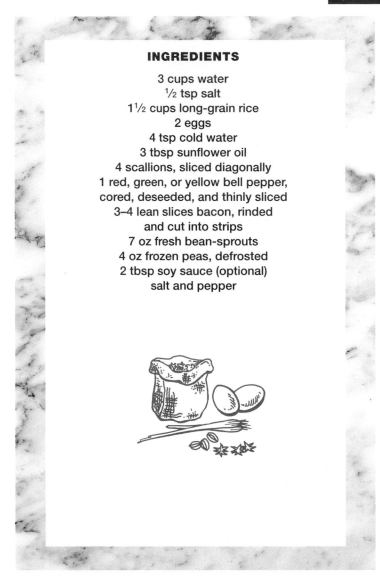

INGREDIENTS

3 cups water
½ tsp salt
1½ cups long-grain rice
2 eggs
4 tsp cold water
3 tbsp sunflower oil
4 scallions, sliced diagonally
1 red, green, or yellow bell pepper, cored, deseeded, and thinly sliced
3–4 lean slices bacon, rinded and cut into strips
7 oz fresh bean-sprouts
4 oz frozen peas, defrosted
2 tbsp soy sauce (optional)
salt and pepper

1 Pour the water into the wok with the salt and bring to a boil. Rinse the rice in a strainer under cold water until the water runs clear, drain well, and add to the boiling water. Stir well, then cover the wok tightly with the lid or a lid made of foil, and simmer gently for 12–13 minutes. (Don't remove the lid during cooking or the steam will escape and the rice will not be cooked.)

2 Remove the lid, give the rice a good stir, and spread out on a large plate or cookie sheet to cool and dry.

3 Beat each egg separately with salt and pepper and 2 teaspoons cold water. Heat 1 tablespoon of oil in the wok, swirling it around until really hot. Pour in the first egg, swirl it around, and leave to cook undisturbed until set. Remove to a board or plate; repeat with the second egg. Cut the omelets into thin slices.

4 Add the remaining oil to the wok and when really hot add the scallions and bell pepper, and stir-fry for 1–2 minutes. Add the bacon and continue to stir-fry for a further 1–2 minutes. Add the bean-sprouts and peas and toss together thoroughly. Stir in the soy sauce if using.

5 Add the rice and seasoning and stir-fry for a minute or so. Add the strips of omelet and continue to stir for about 2 minutes or until the rice is piping hot. Serve at once.

Step *1*

Step *3*

Step *4*

Fried Rice with Shrimp

*Use either large peeled shrimp or tiger shrimp
for this rice dish.*

SERVES 4

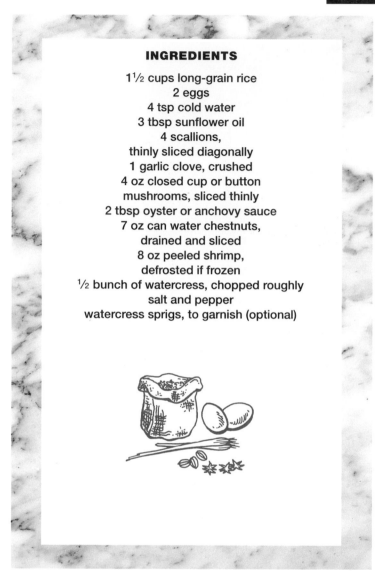

INGREDIENTS

1½ cups long-grain rice
2 eggs
4 tsp cold water
3 tbsp sunflower oil
4 scallions,
thinly sliced diagonally
1 garlic clove, crushed
4 oz closed cup or button
mushrooms, sliced thinly
2 tbsp oyster or anchovy sauce
7 oz can water chestnuts,
drained and sliced
8 oz peeled shrimp,
defrosted if frozen
½ bunch of watercress, chopped roughly
salt and pepper
watercress sprigs, to garnish (optional)

1 Cook the rice in boiling salted water, following the instructions given in Chinese Fried Rice (page 218) and keep warm.

2 Beat each egg separately with 2 teaspoons of cold water, and salt and pepper. Heat 2 teaspoons of oil in a wok, swirling it around until really hot. Pour in the first egg, swirl it around, and leave to cook undisturbed until set. Remove to a plate or board and repeat with the second egg. Cut the omelets into 1 in. squares.

3 Heat the remaining oil in the wok and when really hot add the scallions and garlic, and stir-fry for 1 minute. Add the mushrooms and continue to cook for a further 2 minutes.

4 Stir in the oyster or anchovy sauce and seasoning. Add the water chestnuts and shrimp and stir-fry for 2 minutes.

5 Stir in the cooked rice and stir-fry for 1 minute. Add the watercress and omelet squares and stir-fry for a further 1–2 minutes until piping hot. Serve at once garnished with sprigs of watercress, if liked.

Step *2*

Step *4*

Step *5*

Egg Fried Rice with Chili

This version of fried rice is given extra punch with hot red chilies, scallions, and fish sauce.

SERVES 4

INGREDIENTS

1 cup basmati rice
3 tbsp sunflower oil
1 hot red chili, deseeded and chopped finely
2 tsp fish sauce
3 scallions chopped
1 large egg, beaten
1 tbsp chopped parsley or cilantro
1 tbsp soy sauce
1 tsp sugar
salt and pepper

1 Cook the rice in boiling salted water until tender, about 10 minutes. Drain, rinse with boiling water, and drain again thoroughly. Spread out on a large plate or cookie sheet to dry.

2 Heat the oil in a large, heavy-based skillet or wok until hot. Add the chili, fish sauce, and scallions and stir-fry for 1–2 minutes.

3 Add the beaten egg and stir-fry quickly so that the egg scrambles into small fluffy pieces.

4 Fork through the rice to separate the grains, then add to the skillet or wok, and stir-fry for about 1 minute to mix and heat through.

5 Sprinkle a little of the chopped parsley or cilantro over the rice. Mix the soy sauce with the sugar and remaining chopped parsley or cilantro and stir into the rice mixture, tossing well to mix. Serve immediately.

Step *2*

Step *3*

Step *4*

Fragrant Steamed Rice in Lotus Leaves

*The fragrance of the leaves flavors the rice. Lotus leaves are available
from Chinese shops, but cabbage or spinach leaves can be substituted.*

SERVES 4

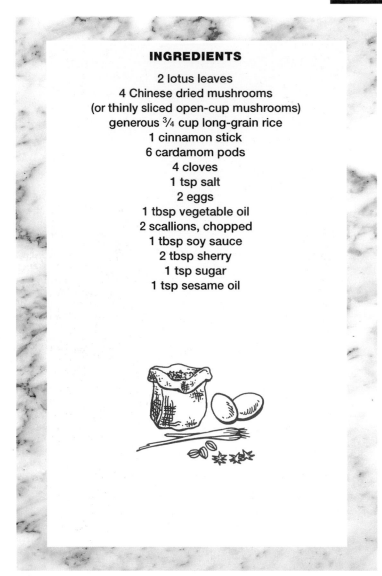

INGREDIENTS

2 lotus leaves
4 Chinese dried mushrooms
(or thinly sliced open-cup mushrooms)
generous ¾ cup long-grain rice
1 cinnamon stick
6 cardamom pods
4 cloves
1 tsp salt
2 eggs
1 tbsp vegetable oil
2 scallions, chopped
1 tbsp soy sauce
2 tbsp sherry
1 tsp sugar
1 tsp sesame oil

1 Unfold the lotus leaves carefully and cut along the fold to divide each leaf in half. Lay on a large cookie sheet and pour over enough hot water to cover. Leave to soak for about 30 minutes or until the leaves have softened.

2 Place the dried mushrooms in a small bowl and cover with warm water. Leave to soak for 20–25 minutes.

3 Cook the rice in plenty of boiling water with the cinnamon stick, cardamom pods, cloves, and salt for about 10 minutes – the rice should be partially cooked. Drain thoroughly and remove the cinnamon stick.

4 Beat the eggs lightly. Heat the oil in a wok or skillet and cook the eggs quickly, stirring constantly, until set; then remove, and set aside.

5 Drain the mushrooms, squeezing out the excess water. Remove the tough centers and chop the mushrooms. Place the drained rice in a bowl. Stir in the mushrooms, cooked egg, scallions, soy sauce, sherry, sugar, and sesame oil. Season with salt to taste.

6 Drain the lotus leaves and divide the rice mixture into 4 portions. Place a portion in the center of each lotus leaf half and fold up to form a package. Place in a steamer, cover, and steam over simmering water for 20 minutes. To serve, cut the tops of the lotus leaves open to expose the fragrant rice inside.

Step *1*

Step *4*

Step *6*

Egg Fried Rice

The rice used for frying should not be too soft. Ideally, the rice should have been slightly under-cooked and left to cool before frying.

SERVES 4

INGREDIENTS

3 eggs
1 tsp salt
2 scallions, chopped finely
2–3 tbsp vegetable oil
3 cups cooked rice, well
drained and cooled
4 oz cooked peas

1 Lightly beat the eggs with a pinch of the salt and 1 tablespoon of the scallions.

2 Heat the oil in a preheated wok, add the eggs, and stir until lightly scrambled. (The eggs should be cooked only until they start to set, so they are still moist.)

3 Add the cold rice and stir to make sure that each grain is separated. Make sure the oil is really hot, otherwise the rice will be heavy and greasy.

4 Add the remaining salt, scallions, and peas. Blend well and serve hot or cold.

Step *1*

Step *2*

Step *4*

Egg Fu-Yung with Rice

Cooked rice mixed with scrambled eggs, Chinese mushrooms, bamboo shoots, and water chestnuts – you can also use up leftover cooked rice.

SERVES 2–4

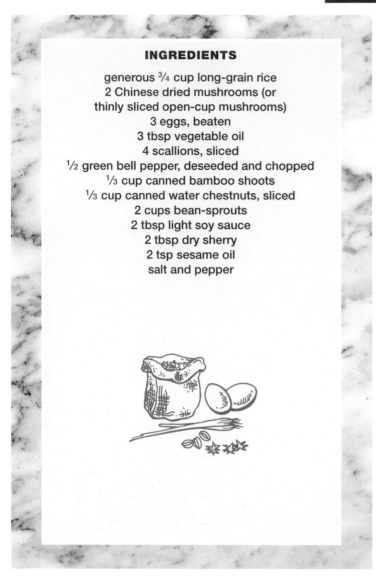

INGREDIENTS

generous ¾ cup long-grain rice
2 Chinese dried mushrooms (or
thinly sliced open-cup mushrooms)
3 eggs, beaten
3 tbsp vegetable oil
4 scallions, sliced
½ green bell pepper, deseeded and chopped
⅓ cup canned bamboo shoots
⅓ cup canned water chestnuts, sliced
2 cups bean-sprouts
2 tbsp light soy sauce
2 tbsp dry sherry
2 tsp sesame oil
salt and pepper

1 Cook the rice in lightly salted boiling water according to the packet instructions. Drain and allow to cool.

2 Place the dried mushrooms in a small bowl, cover with warm water, and leave to soak for 20–25 minutes.

3 Mix the beaten eggs with a little salt. Heat 1 tablespoon of the oil in a wok or large skillet. Add the eggs and stir until just set. Remove and set aside.

4 Drain the mushrooms and squeeze out the excess water. Remove the tough centers and chop the mushrooms.

5 Heat the remaining oil in a clean wok or skillet. Add the mushrooms, scallions, and green bell pepper, and stir-fry for 2 minutes. Add the bamboo shoots, water chestnuts, and bean-sprouts. Stir-fry for 1 minute.

6 Add the rice to the pan with the remaining ingredients. Mix well, heating the rice thoroughly. Season to taste with salt and pepper. Stir in the reserved eggs and serve.

Step *3*

Step *5*

Step *6*

Special Fried Rice with Cashew Nuts

In this simple recipe, cooked rice is fried with vegetables and cashew nuts.
It can be eaten on its own or served as an accompaniment.

SERVES 2–4

INGREDIENTS

generous ¾ cup long-grain rice
½ cup cashew nuts
1 carrot
½ cucumber
1 yellow bell pepper
2 scallions
2 tbsp vegetable oil
1 garlic clove, crushed
¾ cup frozen peas, defrosted
1 tbsp soy sauce
1 tsp salt
cilantro leaves, to garnish

1 Bring a large pan of water to a boil. Add the rice and simmer for 15 minutes. Tip the rice into a strainer and rinse; drain thoroughly, and leave to cool.

2 Heat a wok or large skillet, add the cashew nuts, and dry-fry until lightly browned. Remove and set aside.

3 Cut the carrot in half along the length, then slice thinly into semi-circles. Halve the cucumber and remove the seeds, using a teaspoon. Dice the flesh. Slice the bell pepper and chop the scallions.

4 Heat the oil in the wok or large skillet. Add the prepared vegetables and the garlic. Stir-fry for 3 minutes.

5 Add the rice, peas, soy sauce, and salt. Continue to stir-fry until well mixed and thoroughly heated. Stir in the reserved cashew nuts and serve garnished with cilantro leaves.

Step 3

Step 4

Step 5

Fried Rice & Shrimp

When you've got one eye on the clock and a meal to make, try this!
Quickly made yet simply stunning to look at, its taste belies its simplicity.

SERVES 4

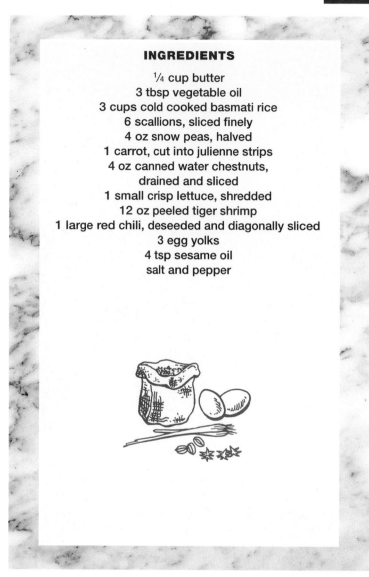

INGREDIENTS

¼ cup butter
3 tbsp vegetable oil
3 cups cold cooked basmati rice
6 scallions, sliced finely
4 oz snow peas, halved
1 carrot, cut into julienne strips
4 oz canned water chestnuts,
drained and sliced
1 small crisp lettuce, shredded
12 oz peeled tiger shrimp
1 large red chili, deseeded and diagonally sliced
3 egg yolks
4 tsp sesame oil
salt and pepper

1 Heat the butter and the oil in a wok or large, heavy-based skillet. Add the cooked rice and stir-fry for 2 minutes.

2 Add the scallions, snow peas, carrot, water chestnuts, and salt and pepper to taste, mixing well. Stir-fry over medium heat for a further 2 minutes.

3 Add the shredded lettuce, shrimp, and chili and stir-fry for a further 2 minutes.

4 Beat the egg yolks with the sesame oil and stir into the pan, coating the rice and vegetable mixture. Cook for about 2 minutes to set the egg mixture. Serve at once.

Step *1*

Step *3*

Step *4*

Rice with Crab & Mussels

*Shellfish makes an ideal partner for rice. Mussels and crab add
flavor and texture to this spicy dish.*

SERVES 4

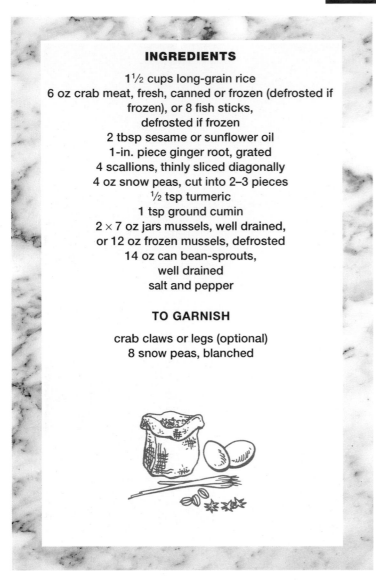

INGREDIENTS

1½ cups long-grain rice
6 oz crab meat, fresh, canned or frozen (defrosted if
frozen), or 8 fish sticks,
defrosted if frozen
2 tbsp sesame or sunflower oil
1-in. piece ginger root, grated
4 scallions, thinly sliced diagonally
4 oz snow peas, cut into 2–3 pieces
½ tsp turmeric
1 tsp ground cumin
2 × 7 oz jars mussels, well drained,
or 12 oz frozen mussels, defrosted
14 oz can bean-sprouts,
well drained
salt and pepper

TO GARNISH

crab claws or legs (optional)
8 snow peas, blanched

1 Cook the rice in boiling salted water, following the instructions given in Chinese Fried Rice (page 218).

2 Meanwhile, extract the fresh crab meat, if using, and flake. If using fish sticks cut into 3 or 4 pieces.

3 Heat the oil in the wok, swirling it around until really hot. Add the ginger and scallions and stir-fry for a minute or so. Add the snow peas and continue to cook for a further minute.

4 Sprinkle the turmeric, cumin, and seasoning over the vegetables and mix well. Add the crab meat and mussels and stir-fry for 1 minute.

5 Stir in the cooked rice and bean-sprouts and stir-fry for 2 minutes or until really hot and well mixed.

6 Adjust the seasoning and serve very hot, garnished with crab claws and snow peas.

Step *2*

Step *4*

Step *5*

Special Fried Rice with Shrimp

Special Fried Rice, sometimes called Yangchow Fried Rice, is almost a
meal in itself. Use completely dry and cold cooked rice for success.

SERVES 4

INGREDIENTS

2 oz peeled shrimp
2 oz cooked chicken, pork, or ham
4 oz peas
3 eggs
1 tsp salt
2 scallions, chopped finely
4 tbsp vegetable oil
1 tbsp light soy sauce
1 tsp Chinese rice wine or dry sherry (optional)
4 cups cold cooked rice

1 Dry the shrimp on kitchen paper. Cut the meat into small dice about the same size as the peas.

2 In a bowl, lightly beat the eggs with a pinch of salt and a few pieces of the scallions.

3 Heat 2 tablespoons of the oil in a preheated wok. Add the peas, shrimp, and meat and stir-fry for about 1 minute. Stir in the soy sauce and wine, then remove, and keep warm.

4 Heat the remaining oil and add the eggs. Stir to lightly scramble. Add the rice and stir to separate the grains. Add the remaining salt and scallions, the shrimp, meat, and peas. Blend well and serve hot or cold.

Step *1*

Step *3*

Step *4*

NOODLE DISHES

In northern China, where wheat grows abundantly, noodles are the mainstay of everyday eating rather than rice. They are temptingly appetizing both in texture and taste. Long noodles are always served at birthday celebrations, and on such occasions the cook will not cut them into shorter lengths because the Chinese believe that the longer they are, the longer and happier will be your life.

There are many types of noodles available, both fresh and dried, made from wheat, buckwheat, or rice flours. They come in fine threads, strings, or flat ribbons, some curled into neat round or oval skeins. You can buy them in oriental food shops or large supermarkets. Like rice, noodles are very versatile – they can be boiled or fried, added to soups, or served plain. Some Chinese like to sprinkle them with salt, pepper, soy sauce, chili sauce, or sesame oil.

Most noodles are prepared in the same way. Because they are precooked as part of the manufacturing process, most noodles need only be soaked in hot water to rehydrate them; sometimes they are boiled or simmered as well. If the packet gives directions on how to cook them, then follow those directions.

Seafood Chow Mein

Use whatever seafood is available for this delicious noodle dish – mussels or crab would be suitable.

SERVES 4

INGREDIENTS

3 oz squid, cleaned
3–4 fresh scallops
3 oz raw shrimp, shelled
½ egg white, beaten lightly
1 tbsp Cornstarch Paste (page 16)
9 oz egg noodles
5–6 tbsp vegetable oil
2 tbsp light soy sauce
2 oz snow peas
½ tsp salt
½ tsp sugar
1 tsp Chinese rice wine or dry sherry
2 scallions, shredded finely
a few drops of sesame oil

1 Open up the squid and score the inside in a criss-cross pattern. Cut into pieces about 1½ x 1 in.

2 Soak the squid in a bowl of boiling water until all the pieces curl up. Rinse in cold water and drain.

3 Cut each scallop into 3–4 slices. Cut the shrimp in half lengthwise if large. Mix the scallops and prawns with the egg white and cornstarch paste.

4 Cook the noodles in boiling water according to the instructions on the packet, then drain, and rinse under cold water. Drain well, then toss with 1 tablespoon of oil.

5 Heat 3 tablespoons of oil in a preheated wok. Add the noodles and 1 tablespoon of the soy sauce and stir-fry for 2–3 minutes. Remove to a large serving dish.

6 Heat the remaining oil in the wok and add the snow peas and seafood. Stir-fry for about 2 minutes, then add the salt, sugar, wine, remaining soy sauce, and about half the scallions. Blend well and add a little stock or water if necessary.

7 Pour the seafood mixture on top of the noodles and sprinkle with sesame oil. Garnish with the remaining scallions and serve hot or cold.

Step *1*

Step *3*

Step *5*

Chicken or Pork Chow Mein

*This is a basic recipe – the meat and/or vegetables can be
varied as much as you like.*

SERVES 4

INGREDIENTS

8 oz egg noodles
4–5 tbsp vegetable oil
4 oz green beans
8 oz cooked chicken breasts,
or pork tenderloin
2 tbsp light soy sauce
1 tsp salt
½ tsp sugar
1 tbsp Chinese rice wine or dry sherry
2 scallions, shredded finely
a few drops of sesame oil
chili sauce, to serve (optional)

1 Cook the noodles in boiling water according to the instructions on the packet. Drain and rinse under cold water. Drain again, then toss with 1 tablespoon of the oil.

2 Slice the meat into thin shreds. Top and tail the beans.

3 Heat 3 tablespoons of oil in a preheated wok until hot, add the noodles, and stir-fry for 2–3 minutes with 1 tablespoon soy sauce, then remove to a serving dish. Keep warm.

4 Heat the remaining oil and stir-fry the beans and meat for about 2 minutes. Add the salt, sugar, wine, the remaining soy sauce, and about half the scallions to the wok.

5 Blend the meat mixture well and add a little stock if necessary, then pour on top of the noodles, and sprinkle with sesame oil and the remaining scallions. Serve hot or cold with or without chili sauce.

Step *1*

Step *3*

Step *4*

Chicken Chow Mein

A quick stir-fry of chicken and mixed vegetables which is mixed with
Chinese egg noodles and a dash of sesame oil.

SERVES 4

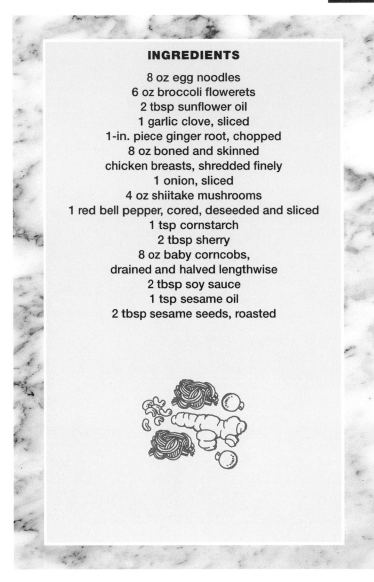

INGREDIENTS

8 oz egg noodles
6 oz broccoli flowerets
2 tbsp sunflower oil
1 garlic clove, sliced
1-in. piece ginger root, chopped
8 oz boned and skinned
chicken breasts, shredded finely
1 onion, sliced
4 oz shiitake mushrooms
1 red bell pepper, cored, deseeded and sliced
1 tsp cornstarch
2 tbsp sherry
8 oz baby corncobs,
drained and halved lengthwise
2 tbsp soy sauce
1 tsp sesame oil
2 tbsp sesame seeds, roasted

1 Put the noodles in a bowl, pour over boiling water, and leave to stand for 4 minutes. Drain thoroughly.

2 Meanwhile, blanch the broccoli in boiling salted water for 2 minutes, then drain.

3 Heat the oil in a wok or large skillet, add the garlic, ginger, chicken, and onion, and stir-fry for 2 minutes until the chicken strips are sealed and the onion softened.

4 Add the broccoli, mushrooms, and red bell pepper and stir-fry for a further 2 minutes.

5 Mix the cornstarch with the sherry, then stir into the pan with the corncobs, sherry mixture, soy sauce, drained noodles, and sesame oil, and heat through, stirring, until thickened. Sprinkle over the sesame seeds.

Step *1*

Step *4*

Step *5*

Singapore-Style Rice Sticks

Rice sticks are long, thin, white noodles. Egg noodles can be used for this dish, but it will not taste the same.

SERVES 4

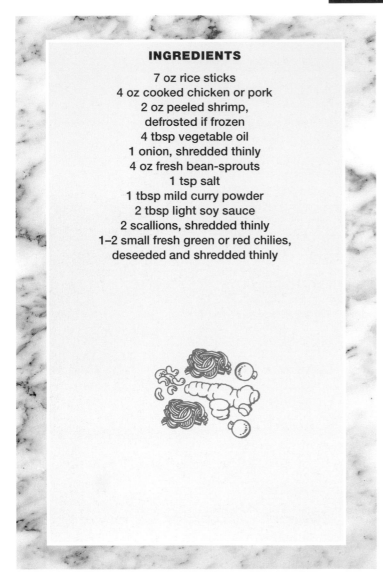

INGREDIENTS

7 oz rice sticks
4 oz cooked chicken or pork
2 oz peeled shrimp,
defrosted if frozen
4 tbsp vegetable oil
1 onion, shredded thinly
4 oz fresh bean-sprouts
1 tsp salt
1 tbsp mild curry powder
2 tbsp light soy sauce
2 scallions, shredded thinly
1–2 small fresh green or red chilies,
deseeded and shredded thinly

1 Soak the rice sticks in boiling water for 8–10 minutes, then rinse in cold water, and drain well.

2 Thinly slice the cooked meat. Dry the shrimp on paper towels.

3 Heat the oil in a preheated wok. Add the onion and stir-fry until opaque. Add the bean-sprouts and stir-fry for 1 minute.

4 Add the noodles with the meat and shrimp, and continue stirring for another minute.

5 Blend in the salt, curry powder, and soy sauce, followed by the scallions and chilies. Stir-fry for 1 more minute, then serve immediately.

Step *1*

Step *2*

Step *4*

Mixed Vegetable Chow Mein

Egg noodles are fried with a colorful variety of vegetables to make this well-known dish.

SERVES 4

INGREDIENTS

1 lb egg noodles
4 tbsp vegetable oil
1 onion, sliced thinly
2 carrots, cut into thin sticks
1⅓ cups button mushrooms, quartered
4 oz snow peas
½ cucumber, cut into sticks
2 cups shredded spinach
2 cups fresh bean-sprouts
2 tbsp dark soy sauce
1 tbsp sherry
1 tsp salt
1 tsp sugar
1 tsp cornstarch
1 tsp sesame oil

1 Cook the noodles according to the packet instructions. Drain and rinse under cold running water until cool. Set aside.

2 Heat 3 tablespoons of the vegetable oil in a wok or large skillet. Add the onion and carrots and stir-fry for 1 minute. Add the mushrooms, snow peas, and cucumber and stir-fry for a further minute.

3 Stir in the remaining vegetable oil and add the drained noodles with the spinach and bean-sprouts.

4 Blend together the remaining ingredients and pour over the noodles and vegetables.

5 Stir-fry until thoroughly heated and serve.

Step *2*

Step *3*

Step *4*

Chow Mein

This is a basic recipe for Chow Mein. Additional ingredients, such as chicken or pork, can be added if liked.

SERVES 4

INGREDIENTS

9 oz egg noodles
3–4 tbsp vegetable oil
1 small onion, shredded finely
2 cups fresh bean-sprouts
1 scallion, shredded finely
2 tbsp light soy sauce
a few drops of sesame oil

1 Cook the noodles in salted boiling water according to the instructions on the packet.

2 Drain and rinse the noodles in cold water; drain well, then toss with a little vegetable oil.

3 Heat the remaining oil in a preheated wok. Stir-fry the onion for about 30–40 seconds, then add the bean-sprouts and noodles, stir, and toss for 1 more minute.

4 Add the scallion and soy sauce and blend well. Sprinkle with the sesame oil and serve.

Step *1*

Step *3*

Step *4*

Homemade Noodles with Stir-Fried Vegetables

These noodles are simple to make; you do not need a pasta-making machine as they are rolled out by hand.

SERVES 4

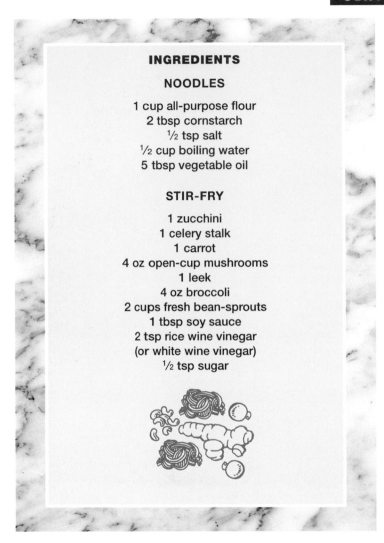

INGREDIENTS

NOODLES

1 cup all-purpose flour
2 tbsp cornstarch
½ tsp salt
½ cup boiling water
5 tbsp vegetable oil

STIR-FRY

1 zucchini
1 celery stalk
1 carrot
4 oz open-cup mushrooms
1 leek
4 oz broccoli
2 cups fresh bean-sprouts
1 tbsp soy sauce
2 tsp rice wine vinegar
(or white wine vinegar)
½ tsp sugar

1 To prepare the noodles, sift the flour, cornstarch, and salt into a bowl. Make a well in the center and pour in the boiling water and 1 teaspoon of the oil. Mix quickly, using a wooden spoon, to make a soft dough. Cover and leave for 5–6 minutes.

2 Prepare the vegetables for the stir-fry. Cut the zucchini, celery, and carrot into thin sticks. Slice the mushrooms and leek. Divide the broccoli into small flowerets, peel and thinly slice the stalks.

3 Make the noodles by rolling small balls of dough across a very lightly oiled counter with the palm of your hand to form thin noodles. Do not worry if some of the noodles break. Set aside.

4 Heat 3 tablespoons of oil in a wok or large skillet. Add the noodles in batches and fry over a high heat for 1 minute. Reduce the heat and cook for a further 2 minutes. Remove and drain on paper towels.

5 Heat the remaining oil in the pan. Add the zucchini, celery, and carrot, and stir-fry for 1 minute. Add the mushrooms, broccoli, and leek, and stir-fry for a further minute. Stir in the remaining ingredients and mix well until thoroughly heated.

6 Add the noodles and toss to mix together over a high heat. Serve immediately.

Step *3*

Step *4*

Step *5*

INDEX

A

almonds, chicken soup with 80
appetizers 19–38
aromatic and crispy duck 116

B

baby corncobs 10
bacon:
    Chinese fried rice 218
bamboo shoots 10
    braised fish fillets 110
    egg fu-yung with rice 228
    golden needles with bamboo
        shoots 206
    noodles in soup 82
    oyster sauce beef 150
    spring rolls 24
    twice-cooked pork 158
    vegetarian hot and sour soup 62
bang-bang chicken 132
barbecue pork (char siu) 38
barbecue sparerib 36
bean sauce 10
bean-sprouts 10
    chicken with bean-sprouts 122
    Chinese fried rice 218
    Chinese hot salad 42
    chow mein 250
    hot and sour duck salad 52
    oriental salad 48
    Singapore-style rice sticks 246
    spring rolls 24
    stir-fried bean-sprouts 204
    vegetable and nut stir-fry 180
beef:
    beef and bok choy 142
    beef and chili black bean
        sauce 144
    crispy shredded beef 152
    ma-po tofu 182
    oyster sauce beef 150
    peppered beef cashew 146
    red spiced beef 148
bell peppers:
    beef and bok choy 142
    beef and chili black bean
        sauce 144
    chicken with bean-sprouts 122
    chicken with bell pepper 128
    Chinese hot salad 42
    five-spice lamb 156
    fried squid flowers 106
    golden needles with bamboo
        shoots 206
    kung po chicken with cashew
        nuts 120
    lentil balls with sweet and sour

sauce 192
    peppered beef cashew 146
    ribs with chili 160
    stir-fried pork with
        vegetables 168
    stir-fried shrimp 90
    twice-cooked pork 158
    vegetable and nut
        stir-fry 180
black bean sauce:
    beef and chili black bean
        sauce 144
    eggplant in 196
    fish with black bean sauce 108
    ribs with chili 160
    tofu and vegetables with 184
black beans 10
bok choy, beef and 142
braising 15
broccoli:
    broccoli in oyster
        sauce 200
    chicken chow mein 244
    Chinese braised vegetables 212
    gingered broccoli with
        orange 198
    peanut sesame chicken 126
butterfly shrimp 30

C

cabbage:
    Chinese braised vegetables
        212
Cantonese cuisine 6–8
carp:
    fish in Szechuan hot sauce 112
carrots:
    Chinese braised vegetables 212
    Chinese hot salad 42
    crispy shredded beef 152
    eggplant in chili sauce 194
    flowers 14
cashew nuts:
    chicken with celery and 138
    kung po chicken with 120
    peppered beef cashew 146
    sizzled chili shrimp 94
    special fried rice with 230
casserole, vegetable and tofu 186
celery:
    chicken with celery and cashew
        nuts 138
    fish-flavored shredded
        pork 162
    peppered beef cashew 146
    red spiced beef 148
char siu 38

chicken:
    bang-bang chicken 132
    chicken and corn soup 78
    chicken chow mein 242, 244
    chicken foo-yung 130
    chicken soup with almonds 80
    chicken with bean-sprouts 122
    chicken with bell pepper 128
    chicken with celery and cashew
        nuts 138
    chicken with mushrooms 136
    Chinese stock 16
    hot and sour soup 60
    kung po chicken with cashew
        nuts 120
    lemon chicken 124
    lettuce-wrapped ground meat 26
    noodles in soup 82
    peanut sesame chicken 126
    Singapore-style rice sticks 246
    special fried rice with shrimp 236
    Szechuan chili chicken 134
    three-flavor soup 72
chili bean sauce 10
chili oil 10
    pork with chili and garlic
        sauce 34
chili powder:
    red spiced beef 148
chili sauce 10
    eggplant in chili sauce 194
chilies 10
    beef and chili black bean
        sauce 144
    braised Chinese leaves 208
    braised pork and tofu 164
    crispy shredded beef 152
    egg fried rice with chili 222
    flowers 14
    kung po chicken with cashew
        nuts 120
    ribs with chili 160
    sizzled chili shrimp 94
    sweet and sour shrimp
        with chili 98
    Szechuan chili chicken 134
Chinese braised vegetables 212
Chinese fried rice 218
Chinese hot salad 42
Chinese leaves 10
    braised Chinese leaves 208
    lemon Chinese leaves 210
    mixed pickled vegetables 50
    oriental salad 48
    stir-fried pork with
        vegetables 168
Chinese stock 16

chop suey, chicken 122
chopping 15
chopsticks 13
chow mein 250
    chicken 242, 244
    mixed vegetable 248
    pork 242
    seafood 240
cilantro 10–11
cleavers 13
corn 10
    beef and bok choy 142
    chicken and corn soup 78
    Chinese braised vegetables 212
    money bags 190
    peanut sesame chicken 126
    corn and crab meat soup 76
cornstarch paste 16
crab:
    baked crab with ginger 102
    rice with crab and mussels 234
    corn and crab meat
        soup 76
crispy seaweed 22
crispy shredded beef 152
cucumber:
    bang-bang chicken 132
    fans 14
    mushroom and cucumber
        noodle soup 56
    pickled cucumber 50
    shrimp stir-fry with
        lemon grass 96
    stir-fried mushrooms,
        cucumber, and smoked
        tofu 188
    sweet and sour cucumber 44

D

deep-frying 15
dipping sauces 17
    crispy wontons with piquant
        dipping sauce 20
duck:
    aromatic and crispy duck 116
    duck with pineapple 118
    hot and sour duck salad 52
dumplings:
    money bags 190

E

egg noodles 11
eggplant:
    eggplant in black bean
        sauce 196
    eggplant in chili sauce 194
    fish eggplant and pork 170

eggs:
  chicken foo-yung 130
  egg fried rice 226
  egg fried rice with chili 222
  egg fu-yung with rice 228
  shrimp soup 74
equipment 13

F
fish and seafood 87–112
  braised fish fillets 110
  fish and vegetable soup 70
  see also carp, sea bass, trout, etc.
fish eggplant and pork 170
fish-flavoured shredded pork 162
fish sauce:
  egg fried rice with chili 222
five-spice powder 11
  five-spice lamb 156
flowers, vegetable garnishes 14
foo-yung, chicken 130
fragrant steamed rice in lotus
  leaves 224
frying 15

G
garlic 11
  eggplant in black bean sauce 196
  lamb and ginger stir-fry 154
  pork with chili and garlic
    sauce 34
garnishes 14
ginger root 11
  baked crab with ginger 102
  gingered broccoli with
    orange 198
  lamb and ginger stir-fry 154
  lemon Chinese leaves 210
  oyster sauce beef 150
golden needles, 11
  golden needles with bamboo
    shoots 206
green beans:
  chicken or pork chow mein 242
  Chinese hot salad 42
  five-spice lamb 156
groundnut oil 11

H
ham:
  three-flavor soup 72
hoi-sin sauce 11
honey:
  barbecue pork (char siu) 38
hot and sour duck salad 52
hot and sour soup 60
  vegetarian hot and sour
    soup 62

I
ingredients 10–12

K
kung po chicken with cashew
  nuts 120

L
ladles 13
lamb:
  five-spice lamb 156
  lamb and ginger stir-fry 154
leeks:
  ma-po tofu 182
lemon:
  lemon chicken 124
  lemon Chinese leaves 210
lemon grass 11
  shrimp stir-fry with lemon
    grass 96
lentil balls with sweet and sour
  sauce 192
lettuce:
  aromatic and crispy duck 116
  hot and sour duck salad 52
  lettuce-wrapped ground meat 26
lime:
  hot and sour duck salad 52
lotus leaves 11
  fragrant steamed rice in 224

M
ma-po tofu 182
meat dishes 141–70
menu planning 8–9
money bags 190
mushrooms:
  braised fish fillets 110
  chicken with mushrooms 136
  dried Chinese mushrooms 11
  egg fu-yung with rice 228
  fried rice with shrimp 220
  lamb and ginger stir-fry 154
  money bags 190
  mushroom and cucumber
    noodle soup 56
  oyster sauce beef 150
  peppered beef cashew 146
  shrimp stir-fry with
    lemon grass 96
  spinach with straw
    mushrooms 202
  stir-fried mushrooms,
    cucumber, and smoked
    tofu 188
  straw mushrooms 12
  vegetarian hot and sour soup 62
mussels, rice with crab and 234

N
noodles 11, 239–52
  chicken chow mein 242, 244
  chow mein 250
  homemade noodles with
    stir-fried vegetables 252
  mixed vegetable chow mein 248
  mushroom and cucumber
    noodle soup 56
  noodles in soup 82
  pork chow mein 242
  seafood chow mein 240
  Singapore-style rice sticks 246

vegetable and nut stir-fry 180
vegetable and tofu casserole
  186

O
oils 11
omelets:
  chicken foo-yung 130
  shrimp soup 74
onions:
  Chinese braised vegetables 212
orange:
  gingered broccoli with
    orange 198
  oriental salad 48
  peanut sesame chicken 126
oriental salad 48
oyster mushrooms:
  shrimp stir-fry with lemon
    grass 96
oyster sauce 11
  beef and bok choy 142
  broccoli in oyster sauce 200
  oyster sauce beef 150

P
pancakes:
  aromatic and crispy duck 116
paprika:
  red spiced beef 148
peanuts:
  peanut sesame chicken 126
  vegetable and nut stir-fry 180
peas:
  chicken foo-yung 130
  Chinese fried rice 218
  egg fried rice 226
  special fried rice with cashew
    nuts 230
  vegetarian hot and sour soup 62
Peking cuisine 8
peppercorns see Szechuan
  peppercorns
pickled vegetables 50
pine nuts:
  spinach with straw
    mushrooms 202
  wonton soup 64
pineapple:
  duck with pineapple 118
  lentil balls with sweet and sour
    sauce 192
plum sauce 11
pork:
  barbecue pork (char siu) 38
  barbecue sparerib 36
  braised pork and tofu 164
  Chinese stock 16
  deep-fried sparerib 32
  fish eggplant and pork 170
  fish-flavored shredded
    pork 162
  hot and sour soup 60
  lettuce-wrapped ground
    meat 26

pork and Szechuan vegetable
  soup 84
pork chow mein 242
pork with chili and garlic
  sauce 34
ribs with chili 160
stir-fried pork with
  vegetables 168
sweet and sour pork 166
twice-cooked pork 158
poultry 115–38

R
radish flowers 14
radish roses 14
red braising 15
red spiced beef 148
rice 217–36
  Chinese fried rice 218
  egg fried rice 226
  egg fried rice with chili 222
  egg fu-yung with rice 228
  fragrant steamed rice in lotus
    leaves 224
  fried rice with shrimp 220, 232
  plain rice 16
  rice with crab and mussels 234
  special fried rice with cashew
    nuts 230
  special fried rice with
    shrimp 236
rice vinegar 11
rice wine 12

S
salads:
  Chinese hot salad 42
  hot and sour duck salad 52
  oriental salad 48
  sweet and sour cucumber 44
  sweet and sour tofu salad 46
salt and pepper, spicy 28
salt and pepper sauce 17
sauces:
  chili and garlic 34
  lemon 124
  piquant dipping 20
  salt and pepper 17
  scallion 17
  sweet and sour 17, 174
  Szechuan hot 112
scallions:
  beef and bok choy 142
  crispy shredded beef 152
  egg fried rice 226
  egg fried rice with chili 222
  eggplant in black bean sauce 196
  eggplant in chili sauce 194
  fish eggplant and pork 170
  fish-flavored shredded pork 162
  five-spice lamb 156
  lamb and ginger stir-fry 154
  lentil balls with sweet and sour
    sauce 192
  peppered beef cashew 146

scallion sauce *17*
stir-fried bean-sprouts *204*
scallops:
    seafood chow mein *240*
    spiced scallops *104*
sea bass:
    fish with black bean sauce *108*
seafood and fish *87–112*
seafood and tofu soup *68*
seafood chow mein *240*
seaweed, crispy *22*
sesame oil *12*
sesame seeds *12*
    peanut sesame chicken *126*
Shanghai cuisine *8*
sherry *12*
shrimp:
    butterfly shrimp *30*
    deep-fried shrimp *28*
    fried rice with shrimp *220, 232*
    shrimp crackers *14*
    shrimp soup *74*
    shrimp stir-fry with lemon
        grass *96*
    seafood chow mein *240*
    Singapore-style rice sticks *246*
    sizzled chili shrimp *94*
    special fried rice with
        shrimp *236*
    stir-fried shrimp *90*
    stir-fried shrimp and
        vegetables *88*
    sweet and sour shrimp *100*
    sweet and sour shrimp with
        chili *98*
    Szechuan shrimp *92*
    three-flavor soup *72*
Singapore-style rice sticks *246*
sizzled chili shrimp *94*
snow peas:
    beef and bok choy *142*
    lamb and ginger stir-fry *154*
    oyster sauce beef *150*
    spiced scallops *104*
soups *55–84*
    chicken and corn *78*
    chicken with almonds *80*
    corn and crab meat *76*
    fish and vegetable *70*
    hot and sour *60*
    mixed vegetable *58*
    mushroom and cucumber
        noodle *56*
    noodles in soup *82*
    pork and Szechuan vegetable *84*
    seafood and tofu *68*
    shrimp *74*
    spinach and tofu *66*
    three-flavor *72*
    vegetarian hot and sour *62*
    wonton *64*
soy sauce *12*
sparerib:
    barbecue *36*
    deep-fried *32*

with chili *160*
spatulas *13*
spinach:
    noodles in soup *82*
    spinach and tofu soup *66*
    spinach with straw
        mushrooms *202*
    wonton soup *64*
spring greens:
    crispy seaweed *22*
spring rolls *24*
squid:
    fried squid flowers *106*
    seafood chow mein *240*
steamers *13*
steaming *15*
stir-frying *15*
stock, Chinese *16*
straw mushrooms *12*
    spinach with straw
        mushrooms *202*
sweet and sour cucumber *44*
sweet and sour pork *166*
sweet and sour sauce *17*
    lentil balls with *192*
sweet and sour shrimp *100*
sweet and sour shrimp with
    chili *98*
sweet and sour tofu salad *46*
sweet and sour vegetables *174*
Szechuan chili chicken *134*
Szechuan cuisine *8*
Szechuan hot sauce, fish in *112*
Szechuan peppercorns *12*
    salt and pepper sauce *17*
    spicy salt and pepper *28*
Szechuan preserved vegetable *12*
    pork and Szechuan vegetable
        soup *84*
Szechuan shrimp *92*

T
tea *9*
techniques *15*
three-flavor soup *72*
tiger lily buds *11*
    golden needles with bamboo
        shoots *206*
tiger shrimp *see shrimp*
tofu *12*
    braised pork and tofu *164*
    braised vegetables with tofu *214*
    hot and sour soup *60*
    ma-po tofu *182*
    seafood and tofu soup *68*
    spinach and tofu soup *66*
    stir-fried mushrooms,
        cucumber, and smoked
        tofu *188*
    sweet and sour tofu salad *46*
    tofu and vegetables with
        black bean sauce *184*
    vegetable and tofu
        casserole *186*
    vegetarian hot and sour soup *62*

tomatoes:
    red spiced beef *148*
    roses *14*
tree ears *12*
    fish-flavored shredded
        pork *162*
trout:
    fish with black bean sauce *108*
twice-cooked pork *158*

V
vegetables *173–214*
    braised vegetables with
        tofu *214*
    Chinese braised vegetables *212*
    fish and vegetable soup *70*
    homemade noodles with
        stir-fried vegetables *252*
    mixed vegetable chow mein *248*
    mixed vegetable soup *58*
    pickled vegetables *50*
    stir-fried mixed vegetables *176*
    stir-fried pork with
        vegetables *168*
    stir-fried seasonal vegetables *178*
    stir-fried shrimp and
        vegetables *88*
    sweet and sour vegetables *174*
    tofu and vegetables
        with black bean sauce *184*
    vegetable and nut stir-fry *180*
    vegetable and tofu
        casserole *186*
    see also bean-sprouts,
        spinach, etc.
vegetarian diet *6*
vegetarian hot and sour soup *62*
vermicelli:
    oriental salad *48*
vinegar *11*

W
water chestnuts *12*
    egg fu-yung with rice *228*
    fried rice with shrimp *220*
    hot and sour duck salad *52*
    sweet and sour shrimp
        with chili *98*
    vegetable and nut stir-fry *180*
wine *9, 12*
woks *13*
wonton skins *12*
    crispy wontons with piquant
        dipping sauce *20*
    wonton soup *64*

Y
yellow bean sauce:
    braised pork and tofu *164*
    chicken with celery and cashew
        nuts *138*

Z
zucchini:
    Chinese hot salad *42*

vegetable and nut stir-fry *180*